Practical Music Education Technology

Practical Music Education Technology

Richard Dammers

AND

Marjorie LoPresti

OXFORD
UNIVERSITY PRESS

OXFORD
UNIVERSITY PRESS

Oxford University Press is a department of the University of Oxford. It furthers
the University's objective of excellence in research, scholarship, and education
by publishing worldwide. Oxford is a registered trade mark of Oxford University
Press in the UK and certain other countries.

Published in the United States of America by Oxford University Press
198 Madison Avenue, New York, NY 10016, United States of America.

© Oxford University Press 2020

CIP data is on file at the Library of Congress
ISBN 978-0-19-983223-1 (pbk.)
ISBN 978-0-19-983221-7 (hbk.)

9 8 7 6 5 4 3 2 1

Paperback printed by Integrated Books International, United States of America
Hardback printed by Bridgeport National Bindery, Inc., United States of America

Contents

Foreword

Students love technology. This statement is obvious to anyone entering a modern classroom. On entering that classroom, it is easy to see students engaged with computers, smart phones, tablets, etc., and the ease with which they use technology is immediately evident. Sometimes it seems that technological confusions that confound and frustrate even the most tech-savvy of teachers are easily explained or fixed by the students in our own classrooms.

Students love music. This statement is also obvious to anyone entering a modern classroom. Students are listening to music through most of their day, sometimes through TV programs, movies, and video games, and often through earbuds or headphones connected (often wirelessly) to their personal devices or computers. Music is an essential part of the human experience, and today's students are interacting with more music, albeit sometimes passively, during any one day than even a decade ago. Students love to talk about their favorite artists, their favorite soundtracks, their favorite genres, their favorite pop songs du jour.

In today's music education classroom, teaching with technology is to be expected. A teacher who puts his foot down and resists technology is now the exception to the norm. Engaging positively with the technology available can have remarkable results in a classroom in terms of students' engagement and achievement.

But technology must not be used just for technology's sake, or it might hinder efforts to improve student engagement and achievement. Herein lie conundrums for many music teachers, especially those who might have graduated from their BEd or MEd degree before the current technological revolution. How do you use technology to enhance what has for decades been a subject taught successfully in non-technological ways, without just checking the technology box on the lesson plan? How do you ensure excellent instruction without risking the fact that the kids might show you up for their superior technological comfort level?

Great music education is a mirror of the students in the classroom. Great music teachers use music which reflects the cultural identity of the students while also extending them beyond that cultural safe place into uncharted territories. Great music teachers use role models with which their students identify easily, so those students can learn that they too can achieve great things without any barrier of race, sex, gender identity, sexual orientation. So also, great music teachers use technology to mirror the students' use of it, and provide ways in which the children can see how they can use their technological comfort to make great music.

Allowing students to lead in the classroom technologically is a leap of faith, but all teachers who have taken that leap have found that this is the best way to engage with the material. You are the music teacher, they are the tech experts, so don't fight that - let them help you with technology and they will be even more receptive to you helping them with music. If the kids know they are your best tech crew, they will be eating the music instruction right out of your hands (figuratively of course).

The Prestissimo series of books is aimed at giving teachers easily-digestible material to help them infuse Music Technology in the classroom. The intention of each volume in the series is that the teacher can choose whichever hints and advice are best for their particular situation, without ever having to worry about digesting or mastering all the material. Each book is written by proven experts in the field, who have done the groundwork and road-tested all the material in their own classrooms.

In this volume. "Practical Music Education Technology", experienced teachers Rick Dammers and Marjorie LoPresti welcome you to an outspread buffet of ideas and resources for using technology in the music classroom. Dr. Dammers and Ms. LoPresti have been leaders of Music Technology education for their entire distinguished careers, and both are recipients of numerous awards for their work with technology in the music classroom, most notably the TI:ME (Technology In Music Education) Teacher of the Year Award - Rick Dammers in 2010, Marjorie LoPresti in 2016. The TI:ME Teacher of the Year Award is the highest achievement in this field.

By leafing through the pages of this book, you will begin to see the scope of resources and ideas available to you. While teachers of performance ensembles will find much here to enhance their music instruction, general music teachers will especially rejoice at the amount of material here suitable for immediate inclusion in their classroom. Dip right in, taste the many dishes in this wonderful buffet, and above all, try these new tastes in your classroom and don't be afraid to ask the students to help with the technology. Students will love these activities, they will be rushing to get to music class every day, they will be telling everyone how cool your class is, and you will have created music lovers for life . . . which is really the reason we all got into this music education business to begin with.

Richard A. McCready
Series Editor

Acknowledgments

I am grateful to my many friends and colleagues in the music education technology community, whose support and collaboration have assisted me with this book and been a valued aspect of my professional journey. I am particularly pleased to have worked on this project with Marj LoPresti, whose passion and energy for improving students' lives through music continues to be an inspiration. I am also thankful for my colleagues in the Rowan University College of Performing Arts, with whom it is a privilege to serve.

My wife Becky Dammers, daughters Abby and Emily Dammers, parents Richard and Florrie Dammers, and parents-in-law Jim and Sue White are a continual source of support, inspiration, proofreading, and love, for which I count myself truly fortunate.

Rick Dammers

When Rick Dammers asked me to join him in this project, I was flattered beyond belief. My thanks to Rick for his consistent support and faith in my abilities.

To the community of educators in TI:ME, thank you for sharing resources that have enabled me to learn at my own pace and welcoming me as a collaborator and conference presenter. Special thanks to my sisters in music education technology: Amy Burns, Barbara Freedman, Cherie Herring, Shawna Longo, Stephanie Sanders, and Katie Wardrobe. You support and inspire me.

To Jim Frankel, Robin Hodson, and the team at MusicFirst: I have learned so much from you and genuinely value your friendship. I am proud to work with you.

To Steve, the center of my heart: The lessons I learned from you cannot be counted. By reading and editing your superior work over the past twenty-five years, I have become a better writer and editor. Your support and understanding have been crucial in bringing this project across the finish line.

Marjorie LoPresti

About the Companion Website

www.oup.com/us/practicalmusictechnology

Practical music technology is an evolving multimedia topic. To supplement this volume, we have prepared materials on a companion website. These materials include links to items referenced in each chapter, supplemental reading, and tutorial videos. To make the most of your reading, please visit the companion website at www.oup.com/us/practicalmusictechnology.

Introduction

Powerful Technology

Take a moment to picture powerful music technology. Visualize it in your mind's eye, walk around it, hear it. What came to mind? Perhaps it was a lab full of the latest computers with new keyboards, an interactive white board, and an adjacent recording studio. Now take a moment to create a new image of powerful musical technology but in which "power" reflects the level of student learning. Perhaps it is a student sitting in the back of a rehearsal room with her headphones plugged into a five-year-old computer that was adopted when new computers were purchased for the school lab. A smile creeps across this student's face as she puts the finishing touches on a duet that she composed for herself and a friend to perform.

The contrast between these images illustrates an important point. The power of technology should not be measured in processing speed (Ghz), storage capacity (GB), or age of equipment. Instead, it should be measured by the outcome for the user, in our case, the musical skills and understandings of our students. The first image, that of powerful music technology with all the bells and whistles of cutting-edge equipment, often is out of reach of most music teachers, but the second and more important image usually is not. Enabling teachers to find affordable paths to powerful uses of music technology is the purpose of this book.

Why Technology?

Using music technology in the classroom is not an inherently good or bad thing. A professional music educator should only utilize music technology when it results in more effective music instruction. Although technology use is not the best way to proceed in every lesson, it increases the tools and possibilities available to music educators. Technology can increase students' and teachers' control over sound, provide teachers with powerful ways to present music, allow for greater individualization of music instruction, and increasingly mediate our broader interactions with music. As a result, technology often provides a means for increasing the effectiveness of traditional teaching approaches as well as allowing for approaches that were not possible before its introduction.

Computer technology can fundamentally change the relation between students and music by giving the students greater control over sound. Through a variety of interfaces, students are allowed to see an entire work in different notational formats yet still are able to edit the smallest details. Much of our musical pedagogy tends to be performance-based, and this has the benefit of requiring students to be actively engaged in real-time action. It can be a drawback, however, when this engagement provides too much (or too little) of a cognitive challenge for a portion of a class. Many software environments now give users the ability to listen to, create, and modify music without specific real-time performance demands. Such active, engaging environments open new dimensions for musical instruction. New pedagogical possibilities range from facilitating student composition and having students run sophisticated recording studios to having students remix and master existing works. This type of control over creating and editing sound opens a shorter, more direct path for students to make musical decisions and provides practical means to incorporate a creative element into the music education curriculum.

The variety of ways in which students can now interact with sound also offers greater opportunities to individualize instruction. The wide variety of software environments now available allows teachers to tailor assignments and levels of support meet particular students' needs. By varying projects according to student readiness, learning style, and interest, music teachers can differentiate their instruction (Tomlinson 1999), a task that can be challenging in many traditional music instruction formats. For example, the use of headphones allows students to work simultaneously on different projects without sonically interfering with other music activities in the classroom. The use of this simple piece of technology significantly expands the teacher's ability to facilitate multiple group or individual projects in the same classroom space. As illustrated in figure I.1, a student and the teacher are working together, another student is intent at the piano, and a third student is playing acoustic guitar without interference by the use of headphones or earbuds.

Technology also gives teachers easier ways to increase the impact of the information they provide in whole-group instruction (as well as individual instruction). By use of a projector teachers can visually reinforce aural concepts of the lesson, and with the recording abilities of the computer, they can provide instant playback of the group's performance. These capabilities allow teachers to work with visual and aural learners, thereby addressing students' learning styles more effectively in lessons or rehearsals. Figure I.2, for example, featuring music teacher Meghan Cabral, demonstrates a best-practice approach in displaying and annotating notation for whole-group instruction.

FIGURE I.1. Students and teacher with headphones

FIGURE I.2. Interactive whiteboard (used with permission from Meghan Cabral, www.anewbandapproach.com)

Another motivation for incorporating technology into music instruction is cultural rather than pedagogical. As a field, education is inherently slow to change. Before becoming a teacher, a person will have been deeply socialized in the educational process for seventeen years or more by his or her experiences as a student. After all of these years of observing teachers, we tend to teach as we were taught. Although this can be beneficial when good teaching practice is transmitted forward through the generations, it can also be a drawback when new approaches are left untapped. Previous generations of music teachers did not use computers and digital technologies, not because they chose not to but simply because the technology was not available. Not only is it a professional educator's responsibility to explore the pedagogical benefits of new technologies, but it is also important that instruction remains current and connected to society. A music classroom that has no technology runs the risk of appearing to parents and administrators as not being relevant to the musical practices of society, or even worse, actually being disconnected from the experiences of the students.

Why Now?

Technology in music education is nothing new. More than fifty years ago the participants in the Tanglewood Symposium looked toward technology with hope (Choate 1968). Early pioneers worked with bleeps and bloops on punchcard-fed mainframe computers and analog synthesizers. With the advent of personal computers came desktop publishing and the arrival of notation software. The arrival of the Internet opened access to vast stores of information. This was followed by the ability to effectively compress and store audio (and video) files, thus turning computers into recording stations and allowing individuals to hold an entire music collection in their pocket.

Although music technology has made vast advances, music education remains largely unchanged. Music teachers generally have positive attitudes toward technology and make frequent use of technology when away from their students, while technology use in the music classroom with students lags behind (Reese 2002; Dorfman 2008; Dorfman and Dammers 2015). There are numerous reasons for this disconnect. Music pedagogy is inherently conservative and resistant to change, because we tend to teach as we were taught. School districts tend to provide general technology support and in-services but not specific music technology support. The biggest obstacles are budget and resources. Often , m usic teachers find that they don't feel they have access to what they need in order to incorporate technology into their teaching.

This account of the untapped potential of technology in music education can be frustrating, yet there are causes for hope. Of the advances mentioned above, the most recent, manageable audio file formats and the ubiquity of the Internet, provide great opportunities for music education. In addition, the price points for hardware and software are dropping radically, increasing the level of access to technology in the music classroom. Synthesizers and software programs that used to cost hundreds if not thousands of dollars are now available for free online. As computing power continues to grow, older machines are still able to handle music computing needs. The end result is that the cost barrier to utilizing technology in music education is disappearing.

Anchor Points

As teachers take advantage of the increased availability of technology in their classrooms, the following three anchor points can be helpful when music teachers are considering how to best utilize technology in their teaching.

Student Learning First

Decisions about technology should always flow from asking how student learning can best be supported, as opposed to asking, "How can I use technology?" Technology is only valuable to the extent to which it can support learning. The specifics of how to approach music technology will vary according to learning objectives and the students involved.

Using Just Enough Technology to Get the Job Done

It is easy for instruction to become focused on teaching students how to utilize a specific piece of software. Although in some instances this can be appropriate, most often this approach serves as a distraction from musical objectives. In five years, the software in question probably will look significantly different or may be totally obsolete, making this learning less valuable for students. The fundamentals of music, however, will be relatively unchanged. Teachers should provide just enough technology instruction in any given software environment to allow students to accomplish their musical task.

You Do Music, Students Do Technology

A phrase borrowed from David Williams, "You do music, students do technology," flows from the previous idea and is important for several reasons. Some teachers find teaching with technology intimidating because their students may be more fluent in current technological environments. Rather than view this as a negative, teachers can feel relieved when they realize that it is not a problem if some students are more technologically adept than they are. The teacher's role is to provide musical guidance, and this role is central and secure. If a student is more technologically proficient, she can be asked to help others, and the teacher's standing as the musical expert in the class is not weakened.

Getting Started

One aspect of music education that will not change is the critically important role of the music teacher in facilitating music learning. As powerful technological tools become available and affordable, it is still the teacher who must find the best ways to utilize the tools to support student learning. This requires a teacher to try something new. The following chapters are organized to provide suggestions for technologies and strategies for teachers to experiment with and implement. With all of the competing demands placed on teachers, maintaining a focus on implementing technology-based teaching strategies requires a commitment to exploring change. This change can be made manageable, however, by focusing on one aspect of technology at time. There is no need to try every technology or idea in the book (in fact, that would probably be ill advised). A wiser approach is to try one or two ideas, refine the strategy to fit your needs, and when it has become a regular aspect of instruction, try another strategy. This book presents starting places that are affordable, but there are other wonderful opportunities provided by more expensive technologies. For teachers seeking such equipment, the most effective advocacy for investment in music technology is to show its transformative power for students working with it. The strategies provided in this book provide a good starting point toward that end as well.

Integrating music technology into instruction is almost always a teacher-initiated process, as it should be. Examining and implementing technology in a manner best suited to his or her students can and should be an empowering experience for the teacher. The information in the following chapters provides a starting point for this process, but the central ingredient will always be the music teacher.

References

Choate, R. (Ed.). (1968). *Documentary report of the Tanglewood symposium*. Washington, DC: Music Educators National Conference.

Dorfman, J. (2008). Technology in Ohio's school music programs: An exploratory study of teacher use and integration. *Contributions to Music Education, 35*, 23–46.

Dorfman, J. & Dammers, R. (2015). Predictors of Successful Integration of Technology into Music Teaching. *Journal of Technology and Music Learning 5*(2), 46–50.

Reese, S. (2002, September). *Trends in technology in school music programs: A four-year study*. Paper presented at the meeting of the Association for Technology in Music Instruction, Kansas City, MO.

Tomlinson, C. A. (1999). *The differentiated classroom: Responding to the needs of all learners*. Alexandria, VA: Association for Supervision and Curriculum Development.

Technology in the Music Classroom

Most educators approach music technology with a valid and important question: *What can technology do for me and for my students?* This chapter provides an overview of the many answers. In many cases, technology is a means to increase student engagement, enhance and deepen musical learning, and extend music learning beyond the boundaries of the classroom. Technology is never an end in itself and should be used when it is the best way to achieve a specific goal for a particular set of learners. Several models for considering the integration of technology in educational setting are discussed below.

At a concrete level, technology allows the creation, control, storage, organization, and distribution of information, as well as collaboration. For musicians, this information includes sound and musical notation. Because computers and web-based applications have become more powerful than in the past, they allow for greater control of sound, making them increasingly useful in musical activities. Whether used to prepare classroom materials, to lead a class or rehearsal, or to direct student activities, technology can support all aspects of musical learning. Below are a few examples of how technology can support a wide range of learning activities in music, directly or indirectly, as related to commonly used standards for arts education.

Connection to Learning Standards
Performing
Singing and performing on instruments are often central to music education. Notation software supports this goal indirectly by democratizing the ability to print music for performance. Whether by expanding repertoire or by allowing music teachers to write custom exercises for their students, technology strengthens music performance instruction, and

ultimately student achievement. The combined use of projection tools and notation software further democratizes the rehearsal room by giving the director the ability to share the score with student performers.

A promising development is the ability of technology to accompany performers. Software and online applications can provide a tonal and metrical context that greatly enriches practice sessions and performances. Likewise, improvements in practice and performance evaluation software provide students with reliable real-time feedback about individual performance in the practice room.

Increasingly, technology provides new instruments for performance. With the advent of free or inexpensive apps, many phones may now become instruments. This expansion of availability of instruments may not be very comfortable for traditionalists, and surely we will not see music majors specializing in cell phone performance soon. With the exception of the human voice, however, *all* instruments were new technology at some point in human history. The widespread proliferation of approachable, accessible instruments is surely a welcome development for music educators, and one that will require a pedagogical paradigm shift in the future.

Creating

Of all the areas of musical engagement, the creation and composition of music is most transformed by technology. Easy control and immediate sound realization simplify the process of creating a musical work. Whether supported through notation software, basic recording software, sequencers, or looping software, a wide variety of options exist for a great variety of potential composers. Many of the available platforms provide a high degree of scaffolding in the form of extensive sound libraries and templates.

Improvising

As with musical performance, technology can support improvisation by providing a customizable practice and performance environment. This customization is particularly important for improvisers, for whom interaction with the musical context is central to the activity. The ability to change the tempo or key or to simplify the chord changes is of great benefit. In addition, the ability to control the speed of recordings of other improvisers without changing the pitch facilitates the transcription of their work.

Reading, Analyzing, and Describing

From flashcard-style drill-and-practice websites to programs that facilitate the notation of music by students, technology offers new ways to help students learn to read and write standard music notation. Free online music notation platforms with intuitive interfaces provide the level of accessibility that learners need for success. Newer web-based sight-reading platforms facilitate the growth of music reading abilities via generation of customized exercises for any level of music reader on any instrument.

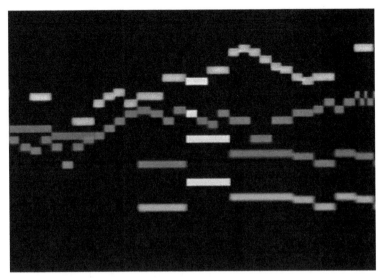

FIGURE 1.1. Screen shot of a Bach fugue as an electronic piano roll

Increasingly, graphic music notation is the standard in the commercial music production realm. Experienced musicians as well as novices need and can benefit from becoming comfortable with piano roll–style notation. In the classroom, students who don't read music can utilize programs with such graphic notation to intuitively and actively analyze musical pieces. Picture a student loading a MIDI file of a Bach fugue and using the piano roll notation to locate and isolate each occurrence of the fugue subject (see figure 1.1).

Online forums, learning management systems, wikis, and word processing software provide helpful support for students who keep listening journals. A plethora of online discussions, podcasts, and videos provide a vast library of reliable, accurate source material for teachers. Many of these resources also provide valuable models for students to understand how to describe music with a meaningful level of detail.

Evaluating

A prerequisite to evaluating musical performances is listening. Complete online music libraries are available for little or no cost, allowing access to a wealth of resources for students. Some music listening subscription services allow users to create curated playlists, enabling teachers to tap a wide range of listening excerpts. In the rehearsal room and in performance settings, freely available recording technology makes it simple to allow students to hear and evaluate their own performances.

Connecting to Other Subjects

Students' musical understanding increases when the music being studied is placed in context with other art forms, with its historical setting, and with concepts from other academic disciplines. With the explosion of information online, it has become increasingly easy for music educators to gather and present information that helps their students make these connections. Further, STEAM (Science, Technology, Engineering, Arts, and Mathematics) initiatives in many schools provide an imperative for music educators to connect musical learning and knowledge to other disciplines, particularly to the technology and engineering that underpin music creation.

Legal and Pedagogical Considerations

Broadly speaking, technology changes the way in which individuals interact with music, with each other, and with the world around them. These changes also have benefits and implications for music educators. Carefully considering these changes will allow teachers to reap the benefits of improved pedagogy while avoiding unintended negative consequences. Among concerns for educators are legal requirements to protect student identity, appropriate choices of technology relative to the learning objectives, and their own ability to keep up with an ever-evolving technology landscape. Legal, pedagogical, and pragmatic issues should be considered while exploring and prior to adopting any new technology for use in the classroom.

Free Versus Subscription Software and Services

Social media, streaming services, and the preponderance of free music and music apps provide wonderful opportunities. YouTube alone can serve as a valuable teaching tool. Many schools block its content, however, owing to the possibility of students' viewing material that is not school-appropriate. Social networks provide music sharing, as well as the danger of copyright violation and risks to student privacy. Free websites and apps often require that students provide an email or other personal information, also compromising their online privacy. Although free material may be appealing, educators are bound by laws that protect student privacy and ensure access only to educationally sound materials. Additionally, school districts have a duty to be able to monitor and supply records of communications between students, their teachers, and among staff members. Laws requiring these aspects of due diligence include the following:

- The Children's Online Privacy and Protection Act (COPPA) requires parental consent for collection of any information about Internet users under age thirteen and precludes the collection of user data without consent.
- The Children's Internet Protection Act (CIPA) requires educational institutions receiving E-rate funding to utilize filters and firewalls to protect students from inappropriate material.
- Freedom of Information Acts (FOIA), passed by some US states as Open Public Records Acts (OPRA), require public institutions such as schools, to access and share

records including communications between teachers, students, and other school personnel upon request.

Scaffolding

Most music software is designed to simplify and facilitate users' interactions with music. Music production programs, or digital audio workstations (DAWs), include libraries of sounds and musical excerpts such as drumbeats and melodic loops. Notation programs include intuitive interfaces, simple input with devices such as keyboards, and editing tools. Multiple DAWs and notation programs exist for almost every age group and experience level for little or no cost. Commands and shortcuts such as use of the spacebar to play or stop have become standardized across programs and web-based applications. These simplified interfaces allow educators to provide scaffolding for their students. By pairing students with a software environment that matches their skills and abilities, music educators can ensure an appropriate level of challenge and a higher rate of successful musical learning.

Whereas the ability to scaffold provides opportunities for improving instruction, it also requires that music educators provide enough challenge to keep students engaged. Teachers must be able to discern how much of the musical product reflects the student and how much reflects the technology. For example, two students might turn in a composition as an audio file. One composition, created entirely of preexisting loops in GarageBand, might sound better but reflect less musical cognition than the other, which was played into a sequencer by the second student.

Expanding the Classroom

Via the Internet, technology allows music educators to expand their classrooms beyond their class period and beyond the walls of the classroom. Very few music educators find themselves with a surplus of instructional or rehearsal time. In fact, most struggle with the opposite problem and are forced to decide which learning objectives to eliminate owing to lack of time. Technology increases the types of activities that teachers may assign to music classes, many of which are available to students outside of class. For example, using a wiki or learning management system, students can explore websites containing information about historical periods, composers, and artworks related to the pieces being performed or studied in class. Online discussion forums provide opportunities for student discussion and interaction beyond the traditional school day. Many platforms offer the teachers the ability to set up an easily graded online quiz. Cloud-based software can provide supplemental instruction, support for music practice, and opportunity for music composition. All of this can be done at little or no cost and without sacrificing a minute of rehearsal time.

students collaborating on laptop. Photo by author.

Educational Technology Frameworks

It is also helpful for teachers to reflect on their use of technology in the context of their own teaching practice. The Triple E, SAMR, and Technological, Pedagogical, and Content Knowledge (TPACK) models provide helpful frameworks for such reflection and provide a connection to use of technology in other disciplines. Further, the ability of music educators to relate their technology needs to school administrators in terms of these frameworks may provide much-needed rationales for adequate funding and equipment.

Triple E

The Triple E model, developed in 2011 by Liz Kolb at the University of Michigan School of Education was created to address the desire of K–12 educators to bridge research on education technologies and teaching practice in the classroom. The three Es represent three primary purposes for technology in school settings: to engage, enhance, and extend (see figure 1.2).

Some technologies such as practicing software promote engagement via a gamelike environment. Many technologies enhance learning by offering customized, differentiated instruction and by adding dimensions such as multimedia illustration of topics.

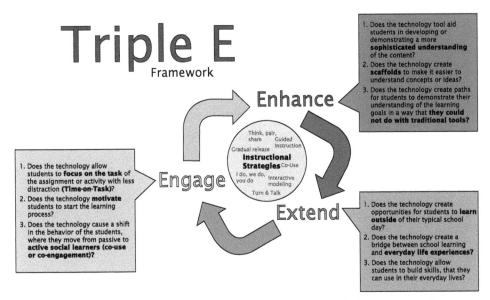

FIGURE 1.2. The Triple E framework (image source: https://www.tripleeframework.com/framework-models.html

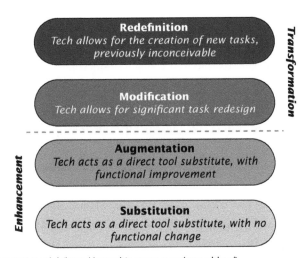

FIGURE 1.3. The SAMR model (http://www.hippasus.com/rrpweblog/)

Technology can extend the boundaries of the classroom by providing a round-the-clock learning environment that students can access outside school.

SAMR

The SAMR model, developed by Ruben Puentedura and shown in figure 1.3, examines technology use in the context of past teaching practice. The name is drawn from four categories (Substitution, Augmentation, Modification, and Redefinition). The "S" and "A" categories reflect uses of technology that enhance traditional teaching practice, while the

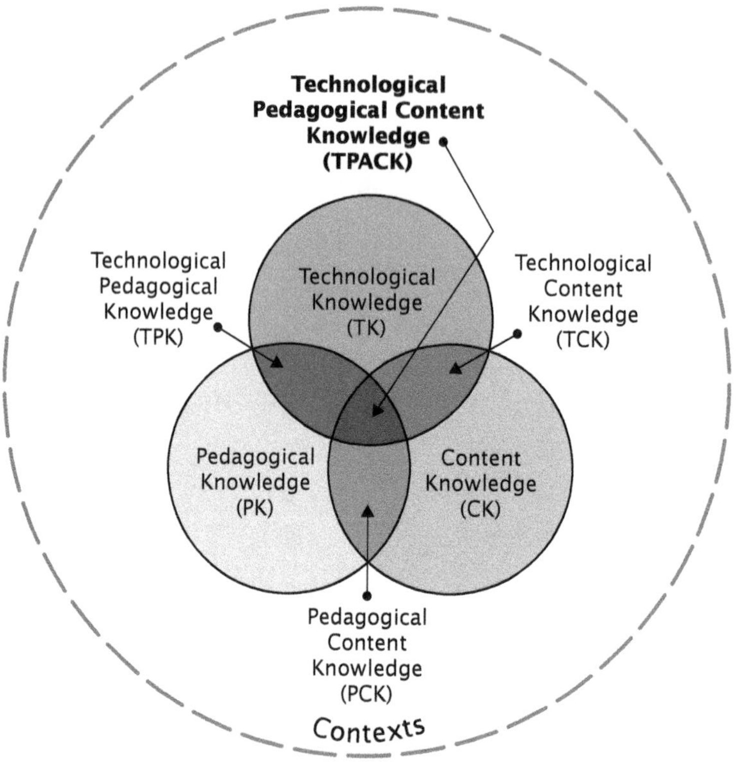

FIGURE 1.4. Graphic showing the contents of TPACK (http://tpack.org)

"M" and "R" categories reflect uses that transform teaching practices into areas that were not possible before. Some examples of these practices follow.

Substitution: Students use an online practice journal instead of a paper-and-pencil journal.

Augmentation: Students engage in peer evaluation, coaching, and critique of practice habits and strategies though review of online practice journals via collaboration features of online documents.

Modification: Students add audio or video recordings to online practice journals to further document progress and elicit meaningful, specific feedback from classmates and the teacher.

Redefinition: Students engage in online practice and critique sessions via video conferencing applications such as Skype, Google Hangouts, Zoom and Whereby .

TPACK

The TPACK framework is useful for thinking about a teacher's knowledge of and use of technology. This model, developed by Matthew Koehler and Punya Mishra and shown in figure 1.4, explores the interaction between technological practice, pedagogical practice, and content knowledge. For example, the ability to utilize email is technological knowledge that does not involve pedagogy or content. Knowing how to tune a string instrument is an example of content knowledge. The ability to teach students to identify beats that occur when a unison note played by two instruments is out of tune is an example of pedagogical content knowledge. The skill of teaching students to employ the tuner in SmartMusic is an example of knowledge that exists in the overlapping areas of TPACK. (For a more extensive list of TPACK music activity examples, please see Bauer, Harris, and Hofer 2012). Generally speaking, the most powerful applications of technology in music education are uses of technology that engage and support pedagogical practice that relates to content (music).

In summary, advances in technology offer supportive or transformative strategies that support musical learning in each of the areas identified in the National Standards for Music Education in the United States. However, technology does more than expand control over information, or support our traditional pedagogy. By changing the ways in which we engage with information and technologies, it also nurtures broader, if more abstract evolution in pedagogy and music education.

Reference

Bauer, W. I., Harris, J., & Hofer, M. (2012, June). Music learning activity types. Retrieved from College of William and Mary, School of Education, Learning Activity Types Wiki: http://activitytypes.wm.edu/MusicLearningATs-June2012.pdf.

2

Classroom Settings

Physical settings and available technology vary widely among schools, types of music classes, and grade levels. Elementary and middle school music classrooms typically are held in standard size classrooms, where open space for singing games and movement activities competes with storage space for musical instruments. Some teachers at these grade levels travel between classrooms or schools. Intermediate and high school music classrooms occupy larger spaces, but tend to be configured primarily for music rehearsal by large groups of students. This chapter discusses approaches to utilizing technology in these typical music room settings. It is important to consider who will be using the technology, be it a teacher using the computer to lead class activities or rehearsals, individual students using the devices apart from other class activities, or entire classes simultaneously using multiple devices.

In most of the scenarios described here, one or more computers or devices are involved, along with peripherals such as speakers, projection systems, interactive whiteboards (IWBs), and document cameras. Purchased new, items needed to outfit a basic teacher station can cost as little as $150 and run into thousands of dollars when IWBs and other devices are added. As a matter of course, however, at least one computer station is made available in a classroom with basic technology integration. By making effective requests to school- and district-based instructional technology departments, teachers generally can acquire additional equipment over time without cost to the music department. Use of older computers and peripherals no longer needed in other departments can supplement the technological capabilities of the music instruction space.

Leading Classroom Activities

Teacher Station

A desktop or laptop computer paired with an LCD projector and external speakers can be a powerful tool for teachers to use in leading a general music class or a rehearsal. From

FIGURE 2.1. Score projection. Photo courtesy of Michelle DaGrosa. Used with permission.

allowing the teacher to post the day's rehearsal order, project the conductor's score, or present web-based information about a composer to having students notate and perform a simple piece or listen to an exemplar recording, these stations offer simple ways to provide aural and visual reinforcement to one's pedagogical objectives. Figure 2.1 shows a simple score being projected in front of an ensemble.

Placement of a teacher station usually requires finding a balance between placing the computer in a location that is accessible by the teacher but not intrusive. This is an important balance. If the computer is too far away or requires the teacher to turn his or her back to students, its usefulness is decreased. When the station is ideally placed, the teacher's activity should be a seamless and transparent part of instruction. Considerations in placing a teacher station include access to power, connections to the projector, and in some cases, wired connection to the Internet. Advance planning, in conjunction with careful wiring, can usually allow for a teacher station be placed in the optimal location.

Recording Station

Like teacher stations, recording stations are set up in order to give teachers or others an ever-present, simple way to record the students' music. Some stations may have an external microphone and may be connected to external speakers. The computer that powers a recording station does not need to be the most recent model; it can be an older computer adopted from an area elsewhere in the school building where it is no longer in use. As long as the computer has a gigabyte or more of free memory, the computer may be a useful tool for making simple classroom recordings. Making recordings for release and production is another matter that usually requires equipment and software beyond the "cheap or free" focus of this book.

The recording station should be placed far enough from the students that the built-in or external microphone can record the full group without distortion (which also requires adjusting the recording level, discussed in Chapter 5). When using an external microphone, a permanent placement via microphone stand or ceiling mounting is preferable because it allows the recording station to be ready to use with requiring setup each time.

Portable Stations

Travelling within or between schools can be an impediment to using technology to lead classroom activities. One solution is to have a desktop computer available in each space. In a situation where the music teacher is working in spaces used for other classes (for example, travelling between elementary classrooms), computers may already be present in each space. With the advent of cloud computing, in which files and resources reside on the Internet, such stations are increasingly useful to traveling music teachers. Portable flash or external hard drives can increase the functionality of these computers. In "art on a cart" situations, it may be possible to include computers, tablets, or projectors on the cart.

As more schools adopt Chromebook and tablet technologies, music educators must advocate for inclusion in this technology integration. Increasingly, schools are issuing such portable devices to each teacher and student. In some circumstances, student devices are housed in a cart, reserved for use in "academic" classes. Many free or inexpensive cloud-based music software solutions that run on these devices are readily available. Such cloud-based and tablet-specific music applications have become quite robust, and they synch automatically to online storage. Music teachers can put the power of these free and inexpensive tools into students' hands easily to provide scaffolding for deeper learning, creativity, and differentiated instruction. Integration of these applications into classroom practice is discussed in later chapters.

Student Use

Although teachers' use of technology can significantly empower them to expand possibilities for instruction, direct student use of technology has the greatest potential for music instruction. This immediately poses the question of the ratio of students to computers. A one-to-one ratio is generally optimal, but groups of students working with a computer, Chromebook, or tablet is a viable option as well. Another consideration is whether the devices will be facilitating the learning of the whole class at once or if the technology station is used by a portion of the class at any given time.

Computer Stations

When facilities and classroom space permit, setting up a single station or a small number of computer stations at the periphery of the classroom is a feasible approach to integrating music technology. These stations can facilitate composition projects, as well as projects that provide knowledge about music. In instrumental classrooms, having a computer station can provide an alternative activity for students whose instruments are being repaired or who can't play because their braces were just tightened. Since other musical activities are going on in the classroom, headphones (and a headphone amp or jack splitter) can be useful in isolating the sound coming from the station. Ideally, these stations should be placed with the screens facing toward the front of the classroom, allowing the teacher to monitor the computer use.

Practice Room Stations

Computer-enhanced practice rooms offer two important advantages: the ability to provide accompaniment and the ability to record. Providing accompaniment via programs like Band-in-a-Box and SmartMusic can greatly enriches and improves the efficacy of student practice. Providing students with the ability to record themselves with a program like Audacity allows them to evaluate and analyze their own performance. It can also facilitate individualized assessment for ensemble classes. As with computer stations, monitoring student use of the computers is important, particularly if the computers have Internet access.

Laptop, Chromebook, or Tablet Carts

The portability of laptops and tablets can ameliorate space constraints and ensure that the portable lab is utilized to its full potential. Laptops can be particularly useful in performance ensembles because their small size allows technology to be integrated easily into the ensemble setup. Portability can also be a drawback, however, because it is easier for such lightweight devices to be lost or stolen. This risk can be minimized with thorough check-in and checkout procedures.

General Computer Lab

In many schools it is not always possible to have a dedicated music technology lab, as shown in figure 2.2, but that does not mean that one-to-one computing (or whole-class utilization of computer labs) is not a possibility. With the advent of web-based programs (cloud computing, discussed in Chapter 3), general school computer labs have become increasingly useful for music teachers. Such labs can be particularly important for creative projects, in which a low ratio of computers to students is necessary for students to be able to explore their creativity. Web-based resources including notation software, informational sites, collaboration spaces and webpages, and web-based recording are often free. Thus music classes can use the lab without imposing on school technology personnel in terms of support (installing software) or funding (the need to purchase a license).

FIGURE 2.2. Music lab at East Brunswick High School. Photo by author.

Away from Class

Technology also offers the opportunity to extend the classroom in terms of both time and space. Through the creation of a class website or online presentations, music teachers can provide information and recordings, facilitate discussions, and support assignments outside of class. Given the limited amount of time in most elementary music classes and in most performance classes, this found time can be a boon. If students have access to the Internet outside of class or rehearsal time, the need for providing a large number of devices is resolved. If one or more students do not have access to a computer and the Internet at home, however, the teacher will need to work with colleagues in the school to help bridge the digital divide with reserved time in the school media center or with the loan of school-owned devices overnight. A "plan B" such as an alternate assignment may also be necessary for students who are not allowed by their parents to access the Internet. Students in either of these situations should be supported with thoughtfulness and respect.

3

Cloud Computing

Cloud Computing and Music Education

The term *cloud computing* though it has become increasingly common, usually is used in terms of commercial or personal productivity and may seem far removed from the music classroom. In actuality, the move to "the cloud" has far-reaching positive implications for music education. By means of increased access and reduced costs, cloud computing dramatically increases the number of music teaching situations in which it is feasible to incorporate technology.

Simply put, *cloud computing* refers to situations in which the software program and files are not on the computer but instead are hosted on a remote server accessed via the Internet. In cloud computing, the computer used becomes less important because it no longer stores the program (other than the Internet browser) or the files. The particular operating system for the computer is also less important, since the cloud programs run within the web browser and not the operating system. For example, a person might use a cloud application on a Macintosh computer at school and on a PC at home without any differences. The files are stored remotely, so the user can access them any time he or she on the Internet.

Advantages

Cloud computing greatly increases music teachers' and students' access to music technology both at school and at home. Prior to the advent of cloud computing, a composition unit, for example, would require a music teacher (without a dedicated lab) to work with the school's tech staff to install software on each station in the school computer lab. Files would need to be stored on each individual station or on the school's server, and students would not be able to work on the composition outside of school. When working in the cloud, no preparation of the lab is necessary. The students can even use a different lab or computer from one class to the next without any problems, and they can easily access their files in the cloud to continue work outside of class. No work is required of the tech support person (who is often more focused on supporting other academic areas). The flexibility of cloud computing can help solve issues of cost and access that frequently have been barriers for music teachers in the past.

Drawbacks

This method of computing does have a few drawbacks. Many of the cloud computing environments have accounts that are tied to email addresses and so are not always appropriate for use with younger students. It is also important to check the architecture of the site to see what needs to be done to keep student work private (if that is a concern). The remote storage of files means that a unit could be ruined very quickly if a company went out of business and all of the student work disappeared. Internet access can also be an issue. If Internet access is unreliable, cloud-computing approaches may not be viable. These are minor concerns, however, and the advent of cloud computing adds to the ways in which technology can support musical learning.

Examples of Cloud Computing Applications

Cloud computing applications do the same tasks as do traditional applications. The difference is only that the users access the program and stores files on a remote server. Therefore, examples of cloud computing are addressed in succeeding chapters of this book, based on what the application does. A few brief examples are included in this chapter in order to illustrate how cloud computing can serve music educators.

Notation Software

Noteflight

The ability to have students easily notate music in a huge benefit of music technology. Noteflight is the first cloud-based music notation application. With the advent of this program, students can easily notate, listen to, and print their own music on any computer with Internet access. From the teacher's perspective, this also means students can write music in school or at home. Because the program is organized in terms of individual accounts, students can have access to their files on any computer just by signing in to their account. There are some limitations on the free version of Noteflight. Paid versions (which are more expensive than the $150 cost limit that is the aim of this book) include Noteflight Learn, which allows teachers to create their own classroom community, and Crescendo, which has a larger set of available instruments and sounds. Figure 3.1 shows an open score with easy access to menus and formatting tools.

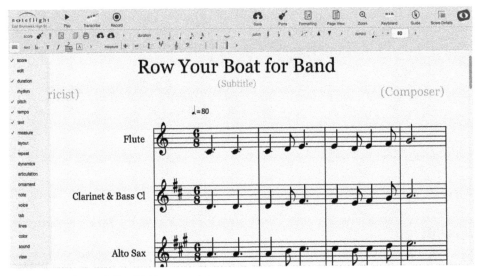

FIGURE 3.1. A sample Noteflight screen shot

The free version of Noteflight works for most student use and many teacher needs. Working in a web browser, the user selects staves for the score and enters notes by pointing and clicking or by selecting the note duration and typing the pitch names. The score can be played using the built-in synthesized sounds or exported as MIDI or XML files. The score and parts can be printed if paper copies are needed. Subscription-based Noteflight Learn, the premium education version, offers learning tool integration (LTI) with Google Classroom and other learning management systems. Noteflight Learn also includes access to free lesson plans, scores, and the functionality to create assignments and group students into classes.

Flat

Flat is robust cloud-based music notation software much like Noteflight. The free version limits users to fifteen scores, which will print only with Flat branding. Flat for Education offers LTI with Google Classroom and other learning management systems if one acquires an annual subscription.

The capabilities of notation software can be put to use in a variety of ways. For example, in a band setting, it is inevitable that a student will need to sit out a rehearsal because of an instrument repair or because his or her braces have been tightened. Perhaps that student's time can be put to a creative and productive use by allowing him or her to use the band room's single computer station to create a melody in the key and style of the music being addressed in class that day. (This is far better than expecting that student to sit silently with nothing to do!)

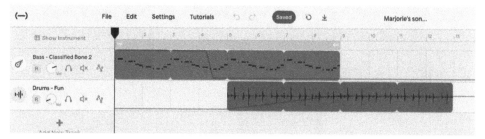

FIGURE 3.2. The Soundtrap interface

Music Production

Soundtrap

Soundtrap is a user-friendly, robust online DAW. The free version allows users up to five projects. Affordable school licensing for a premium version of Soundtrap with LTI is available, as are individual paid subscriptions. The real advantage of Soundtrap is the built-in collaborative features. Students can be logged into the same project on separate devices and in separate locations, much as they can in the Google suite. Soundtrap offers two-way audio and video chat, as well as real-time audio and MIDI recording. Figure 3.2 illustrates Soundtrap's user-friendly interface and clear differentiation of MIDI as a bar graph or piano roll, and audio as a waveform.

Soundation

Like Soundtrap, Soundation is a cloud-based DAW. The free version allows MIDI recording but no live audio recording or audio import. The rather sophisticated virtual MIDI instruments offer the features of a synthesizer. Affordable school and institutional packages provide the full premium version and protection of students' identities.

BandLab

BandLab offers a free online music production studio. In Bandlab for Education, teachers have the option of creating classes and adding assignments. The platform works across all devices, including tablets and phones, and offers real-time collaboration. The interface is similar to those of both Soundtrap and Soundation.

Pro Tools First

Avid's Pro Tools First offers users the opportunity to record, edit, and mix projects with up to sixteen audio tracks for free. This program can be an excellent starting point, but as with many free things, there are significant drawbacks. As expected, this cloud version of a very robust program has limited features. Although it provides an excellent introduction to Pro Tools, it offers cloud storage only. Further, Pro Tools First sessions cannot be opened using a full version of Pro Tools.

Audiotool

If Soundtrap is the online equivalent to GarageBand, Audiotool is the cloud analog to Reason. Through a web browser, Audiotool allows the user to play virtual drum machines, bass synthesizers, and tone matrixes and allows the user to mix and apply virtual effects pedals. In other words, a user can create his own house mix (via 1980s-vintage synths) just by opening this free site. An account is required in order to save work. This site provides a lot of opportunities for creative experiences in popular styles. There is a lot to learn about operating each virtual piece of equipment, so this site is more useful for in-depth experiences, whereas other basic online drum machines such as OneMotion (https://www.onemotion.com/drum-machine) may be more appropriate for younger students or more cursory lessons.

Productivity

Google Tools

Perhaps the most well-known example of cloud computing is Google Docs. The Google suite of programs is very similar to the familiar Microsoft Office suite of programs, all accessed through a web browser. The added advantage is that word processing files, spreadsheets, and presentations can be easily shared and edited by multiple users, and users do not need to worry about transporting the files. Instead, the files are available to that user anytime he or she is online, stored safely in Google Drive. From the Google Drive interface shown in Figure 3.3, users can quickly access files and add new documents. Though not designed to work with music (sound or notation), these tools can be of use for music students and teachers alike. The ability to simultaneously edit a document from two or more different computers can facilitate group work. For example, imagine a band in which each section is responsible for researching and preparing a report on one of the composers whose work the band is performing on an upcoming concert. The online collaborative function of the Google suite allows the students to work together, outside of class, at the same or at different times, to complete the report.

Office 365

Microsoft has moved to a cloud-based model in addition to its time-tested desktop applications. Recent additions to the suite of word processing and presentation software include Sway, a multimedia storytelling tool that easily integrates images, audio, and video. OneNote is an online storage tool like a virtual binder. Teams and SharePoint provide collaboration, communication, and shared cloud storage. OneDrive functions as cloud storage for all of the Office 365 applications. Widely adopted in the business community, the Microsoft suite is being used in an increasing number of schools.

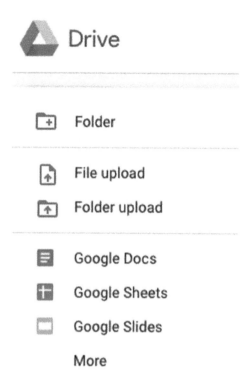

FIGURE 3.3. The Google Drive interface

Dropbox

Dropbox is a free online file storage resource. This virtual hard drive automatically updates on any computer or mobile devices with the Dropbox app or software and is accessible through any web browser. This facilitates the transfer and sharing of any kind of file. The free level of service, Dropbox Basic, provides 2 GB of storage While Dropbox is not the optimal way to deliver files like worksheets or rehearsal recordings to students, it is a useful tool for collaborating with colleagues and for keeping ones' materials organized between multiple computers. For example, imagine two band directors who were roommates in college and now live in different parts of the country. These friends had always been each other's best critics and supporters, and each missed hearing the other's band. Using a shared folder in Dropbox, they now send each other video files of their rehearsals (which they discuss the next time they talk on Skype).

Summary

Cloud computing is an exciting development for music educators. Many powerful programs are now accessible on any computer for free. This eliminates the need for dedicated computer labs and makes it easy for a school computer lab to become useful for music instruction. Cloud computing also allows teachers to make assumptions about what students can access outside of school. Teachers need to vet materials and applications they ask students to access online for appropriateness and legal compliance, but they now can know that students who have Internet access can benefit from the resources described above. As technology continues to develop, connectivity improves, and as we continue to move to mobile computing devices, the opportunities to support musical learning through cloud computing will continue to grow.

4

Notation Software

This chapter discusses traditional and cloud-based notation software. Notation software is an older branch of music technology than other areas simply because computers were able to handle notation before they could effectively process sound. The What You See is What You Get (WYSIWYG) standard began with desktop publishing. The advent of notation software in the 1980s began the What You *Hear* is What You Get revolution, which is still ongoing. Two dominant programs, Finale and Sibelius, emerged from the field and remain competitors today. Recently, cloud-based and open-source options such as Noteflight, MuseScore, and Flat have appeared. Whereas the full versions of Finale and Sibelius are beyond most school budgets, their basic versions are within the $150 range. NoteFlight, MuseScore, and Flat are free. This chapter discusses the capabilities of each title and considerations for using it with students.

Description of Notation Software

Notation software, is essence, is word processing software for music. Its primary purpose is to arrange staves and notes for printing on paper. Users go through the same processes as they would with word processing: entering information, editing, proofreading, adjusting layouts, and printing. Many of the same tools are available, including cut, copy, and paste. As with desktop publishing, notation software greatly expanded the number of people able to print their own music. In years past, if a student composed a piece for the school band, the process of hand copying the parts was a significant barrier to having the work performed. With notation software, this barrier is removed with simply by selecting Print Parts. The ability to easily create printed music has been beneficial for music teachers and is becoming an increasingly important capability for music students.

While there are certainly differences between the affordable notation software options discussed in this chapter and the more costly options, the central process of notating a score is generally the same. The score is laid out with the number and type of staves, meter, key, and tempo. These parameters can be changed and modified later on by accessing user-friendly menus.

The primary aspect of notating a score is note entry—the equivalent of typing in a word processor. There are number of ways to accomplish this in notation software. The most basic programs utilize only the computer keyboard and mouse or trackpad. In this process the user selects the note duration and clicks the pitch onto the staff. In a variant of this process the user types the letter name, and the program adds a note of that duration on the next available beat. In a more advanced process, the pitch is selected from a piano keyboard or controller connected to the computer. Keyboards are used in two different ways. In "step-time" entry the keyboard is used as a replacement for typing the pitch letter name. The user selects the pitch on the piano keyboard and then selects the duration on the computer keyboard, at her own pace. With the other option, "real-time" entry, the user selects a tempo and then performs the part on the piano keyboard. The program takes the MIDI data from that performance and translates it into notation. As discussed below, real-time entry is not an option in the more affordable notation programs.

Another exclusive feature of the more expensive programs is the ability to scan printed music into the programs. There is a time-saving music entry option that is common to all of the notation programs, however: opening MIDI files. The MIDI (Musical Instrument Digital Interface) file format is a standard file format that is read by almost all music software programs. It is the communication protocol and file format that allows communication between musical programs and devices including piano keyboards and sound cards. There are many online repositories of existing MIDI files. For example, the International Music Score Library Project (IMSLP) contains MIDI files for more than three hundred thousand public domain pieces available for download. Although some of these MIDI files were not intended for viewing in notation programs, many, if not a majority, were, and they open very nicely. To illustrate the time savings, imagine a class studying Beethoven and a teacher wanting to have a score or excerpt of the Fourth Symphony. Entering the score by simple note entry would probably not be worth the teacher's time. By comparison, finding a MIDI file of the symphony online and opening it in a notation program would probably take five minutes or less.

Layout

As "music processing" programs, notation editors are used mainly to create legible, pleasing musical layouts. All programs, including free and online options, provide a clean layout for basic scores of up to four staves or instrument parts. "Freemium" options, with very low per-user costs but premium features, like Noteflight Learn allow as many staves as needed. All programs include the ability to add text including title, composer, lyrics, and instructions such as tempo, dynamics, and articulation. Graphics such as repeat signs and expression markings are included. Line breaks and page breaks are easily created and changed. Notation software programs all include the ability to switch from concert pitch to transposed view. Most include the option to change from page layout to "strip view," in which the music flows across the screen without line or page breaks. Higher-end programs such as Finale and Sibelius include the ability to move and customize staff elements and symbols and to import or export graphics.

Playback

The primary purpose of notation software is to print music on paper, but playing back the score is an integral function. This capability allows the user to hear the full work and permits auditory proofreading. In addition to letting the user hear the score while working, the programs allow the final product to become an audio file as well. Notation programs vary in the quality of the synthesized or digital audio clips used to realize the score.

There are certain advantages to the more expensive full versions of Finale and Sibelius. These programs have deep menus that allow more extensive layout options. Perhaps the features that are most advantageous to teachers are the ability to scan in music perform real-time note entry, and, in Finale, create custom SmartMusic files. The typical music teacher does not utilize many of the other features, however, and the more affordable programs have the critical advantage of accessibility by students at school and at home. It is far more important to have a program that students can actually use than to have a program that can check for parallel fifths for you but that students will never see. The basic functionalities of these affordable programs (Finale NotePad and Print Music, MuseScore, Noteflight, Flat, and Sibelius Student) are powerful enough to support both teacher and student use.

Comparison of Programs

Finale Print Music, NotePad, and Reader

One of the two long-standing titles in notation software is Finale. Although the full-fledged version of Finale is more expensive than most school budgets can handle, there are three scaled-down versions of the program: Finale Print Music (annual subscription), Finale NotePad (free), and Finale Reader (free) that do fit within the parameter of afford-ability for schools.

As the name implies, Finale Reader allows the user to open and view Finale files. This program does not allow for editing or creation of original files. Finale NotePad, shown in figure 4.1, allows the user to create files and enter notes by pointing and clicking, as well as by typing. The menu options are provided with simple icons. Limitations include a lack of MIDI entry, a maximum of eight staves, and compatibility with Windows OS only. Finale Print Music has a broader set of capabilities including MIDI note entry and conversion of the file to audio for export , and it allows up to twenty-four staves.

FIGURE 4.1. A sample image from Finale Notepad

MuseScore

MuseScore is free open-source notation software. "Open-source" denotes a program that generally is collaboratively designed to be distributed for free. (Audacity is another example of an open-source music program.) Unlike Noteflight, MuseScore is not cloud-based but, rather, is downloaded to and run on a specific computer. There are versions available for computers running Macintosh, Windows, and Linux operating systems. The current MuseScore 3 is robust, and its functionality and stability rival those of Finale and Sibelius.

As you might suspect, MuseScore does not do everything that Finale and Sibelius can, but it is very functional for basic notation tasks. Notes are entered via pointing and clicking, computer keyboard typing, or step-time entry with a piano. It does not currently allow for real-time MIDI note entry, but it will open preexisting MIDI and MusicXML files. Files (score and parts) can be exported to PDF only. The program supports audio playback using MIDI to audio conversion. Such MIDI to audio playback can also be saved in WAV audio format .

Though not a cloud application, MuseScore does maintain a website for the sharing of program files. The application download link and access to the shared library are available at MuseScore.com. Figure 4.2 shows the MuseScore interface with a free public domain score. MuseScore users should be advised that not all content in the MuseScore peer-to-peer sharing library is in the public domain. Music to be used with students should be vetted by the teacher for copyright compliance.

FIGURE 4.2. Screen shot of MuseScore

MuseScore is an ideal choice for basic notation, especially when multiple copies are needed (for example, for student use). In addition to being free, it can be used when Internet access is unavailable or not desired. It also provides an option for student use at home that does not require students to be online or to link their work to an email address, which is desirable for younger students.

Noteflight

Noteflight is a free online notation program. An example of cloud computing, Noteflight has the advantages of not requiring software to be installed on a computer and being accessible from any computer with Internet access.

All users create an account when using Noteflight, allowing them access to their scores. These scores may be public or private. (Noteflight has an extensive public sharing area for scores.) Working within the web browser, users enter pitches either by pointing and clicking (working within the drop-down menus) or by typing pitch names. Noteflight accepts MIDI signals for step-time note entry but not real-time entry. It does open MIDI and XML files. Playback is through internal synthesizers; Noteflight files can be exported as WAV or MP3 audio files, MIDI files, XML files, or a PDF score. Scores and individual parts can be printed directly from the browser. The sharing feature includes the option to export the file as an embedded code, turning scores into interactive playback elements that function in real time on web pages.

Unlike MuseScore, Noteflight is not open source, and though free, it is a scaled-down version of the paid version of Noteflight Premium. Limitations of the free version include the reduced number of scores a user can store and the variety of instruments available. The full version of Premium, branded Noteflight Learn, allows LTI integration with a specific LMS, creating a closed online learning community for a class. A key feature of Noteflight Learn for school settings is the ability to make any score a template, like a worksheet. This menu option is shown in figure 4.3. This template function enables

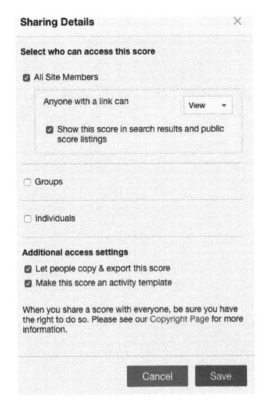

FIGURE 4.3. Noteflight Share menu with template making option

students to make copies of the original score and submit their own work, linked directly to the original provided by the teacher. Applications of this functionality are especially wide-reaching in general music and music theory classes. Annual subscription rates for Noteflight Learn start at $69 for ten users, with additional users costing $2 each.

Sibelius

Sibelius Ultimate, like its longstanding competitor Finale, is far more expensive than the $69 Noteflight Learn, but it does offer affordable scaled-down versions. Sibelius First allows the user to create and read Sibelius scores and create scores with up to four staves for free. It has export options similar to those of the above-mentioned titles. Sibelius limits users to sixteen staves for $5 per month. The full-featured Sibelius Ultimate is $20 or more per month, though educational pricing may make subscriptions for students and teachers affordable on school budgets.

Summary

Although notation software has been available for decades, the appearance of cheap or free versions is a more recent phenomenon that allows students as well as teachers to use

TABLE 4.1. Commonly used music notation programs

Finale (https://www.finalemusic.com) Purchase or subscription	NotePad version free Limited Print Music version, $120 academic price Full version, $99 for students, $350 academic price
Sibelius (https://www.avid.com/sibelius) Purchase or subscription	Sibelius First free for up to 4 staves per score Sibelius, $5/month for up to 16 staves per score Ultimate version, $10/month or $300 perpetual license
MuseScore (https://musescore.com) Software download Option to store and share scores online	Free
Noteflight (https://www.noteflight.com) 100% cloud-based subscription	Limited version, free for up to 10 scores Premium, $8/month or $49/year Learn, classroom edition starting at $69/year for 10 users
Flat (https://flat.io/) 100% cloud-based subscription	Free

notation software. It is now reasonable for teachers to expect that students have access to software with which to write music in standard notation on any computer they use at school or at home. This access has widespread benefits in many music education settings. To help with the exploration and decision processes, table 4.1 provides a snapshot of the options discussed in this chapter.

5

Audio Recording

Overview

As computers have gained memory and faster processors and have begun to use more efficient file formats, they have become able to effectively record, process, and store digital audio. Effective audio recording is no longer restricted to high-end computers that can; older or average computers equipped with free software have this capability. While the ability to record is valuable in many areas of education, it is most important in the music classroom.

Specific strategies and applications for recording audio in the music classroom are included in Chapters 12 and 13. The focus of this chapter is on options for capturing and editing audio to support classroom activities. Though the world of digital recording is complex and often expensive, our focus will be on basic, easy approaches with the aim of facilitating classroom recordings that will support student learning. This goal is attainable with basic equipment and a little practice with the software.

Recording Stations and Equipment

Considerations about a computer recording setup should begin with the space in which classes occur and the available computer equipment. A schedule that involves teaching in multiple spaces may necessitate using a laptop, tablet, field recorder, or other mobile device, whereas a fixed space may allow for the use of a desktop computer. When recording, the device should be located in front of the group at a short distance, depending on the size and volume of the group being recorded. While there is an art to microphone placement, when making basic recordings for class use, simple placement is more than adequate. Prior to capturing a rehearsal or performance, testing the microphone setup is essential. The volume level into the recording device or software should be strong, but not overblown, or *clipped*. Make a test recording with the musicians playing at their fullest volume. If the playback sounds overly loud or distorted, reduce the recording input volume on the computer, handheld device, or in the software settings.

In situations where the teacher's computer station is located in another room, it may be necessary to use a different device for recording. In this case, it may be possible to "adopt" an older computer or other device from elsewhere in the school. A device that is four or five years old will still be more than functional as a recording station. A dedicated computer for recording is preferable because the hard drive can be cleared and used solely to store recordings. Use of cloud storage for recordings may alleviate concerns about losing files when a dedicated device is not available.

Most laptop computers and, increasingly, desktop models have built-in microphones, and these microphones have been increasing in quality over time. They have limitations, but in some instances the built-in microphone is of sufficient quality for classroom and rehearsal recording. Before purchasing any extra equipment, it is certainly worth testing these microphones to see if they are compatible with your device and if the quality is satisfactory.

If the device lacks a built-in microphone, or if it is inadequate, low-cost alternatives are available. One approach is to purchase a USB microphone such as Blue's Snowball (figure 5.1), Blue's Yeti, or Samson's Meteor. Simple and easy to use, these microphones

FIGURE 5.1. A Blue Snowball USB microphone

provide quality input to the recording software. They also allow for greater flexibility of microphone placement, though placement is still limited by the reach of the USB cable.

Setting up a USB microphone is fairly simple. After it is plugged into the USB port of the computer, the microphone will be active. While you do not need to install any software, you will need to check in two places to make sure that the microphone's signal is reaching your recording program. First, you'll need to check the operating system preferences to select your microphone's input. This varies by operating system.) After this is done, you'll need to check the preferences of your recording software as well. It is a good idea to start your program after you plug in your microphones. Typically, software programs will look to see what microphones are available at startup but will not continue to look after startup, so if you plug in a microphone later, the program will not know that the microphone is there.

Many schools and home studios use, quality dynamic or condenser microphones for recording rather than USB mics. They must be connected to the computer through a Digital Interface (DI) box. In such a configuration, the audio signal captured by the microphone flows to the DI box through a standard XLR microphone cable, the kind used in a typical auditorium sound system. The DI box converts the audio signal to 1's and 0's, and sends it to the computer with a USB cable. USB microphones simplify this process, but afford the user less flexibility with regard to placing multiple microphones or achieving optimal microphone choice and placement for a high quality recording.

Portable Recording Devices

Many teachers have access to free and affordable recording options through apps for mobile phones and tablets. Voice recorder apps are available for free on virtually every such device. These function well for basic classroom and rehearsal room recordings.

Many schools have adopted Chromebooks and other styles of netbook. Free recording and editing plug-ins and extensions for the Chrome browser include Twisted Wave and Mic Note. Though the cost of using these types of mobile devices for recording may be low, so is the audio quality. The native microphones on such devices are typically designed for voice and do not have the frequency response needed for quality music recording. Adding an external microphone will greatly enhance fidelity. Such microphones cost between $50 and $80. Affordable audio editing apps such as TwistedWave for iOS and WavePad for Android allow editing and file sharing directly on the mobile device.

Handheld digital recorders (field recorders) such as those made by Tascam and Zoom provide excellent options for making high-quality recordings. These devices record to a flash memory card and can serve as an external microphone for computer. Such field recorders have been dropping in price and will likely continue to do so. Basic models are in the $80 to $120 range. The Zoom H4N shown in figure 5.2 costs nearly to $200 but provides CD-quality recording.

FIGURE 5.2. The Zoom H4N handheld digital recorder

Recording and Editing Software

There are many affordable software programs for making and editing recordings. There is considerable overlap between programs for recording and editing audio with sequencing programs or digital audio workstations. These workstations generally contain built-in loop libraries and function as MIDI sequencers as well as audio recorders. For purposes of clarity, this section will focus on three software titles only.

GarageBand

Apple computers come with GarageBand software, which, in addition to serving as a looping and sequencing program, records live audio. This program has the advantages of being free (to Mac owners), being intuitive to use, and having simple export options, such as sending the recording to iTunes or exporting them as MP3 files. GarageBand has a series of preset recording effects that allows users to intuitively apply changes to their incoming recorded sound without getting into the details. For example, the male voice setting applies a preset equalizer filter to optimize the typical male frequency range and cut high-end noise from the sound. GarageBand's looping and sequencing capabilities allow users to combine their own audio recordings with looping materials and synthesized MIDI sound, enabling students and teachers to incorporate their voice or instrument into their GarageBand compositions.

Mixcraft

On Windows, Mixcraft has similar capabilities, but does not come included on Windows machines; this represents an additional expense ($50). Like GarageBand, Mixcraft has the additional capabilities of being a MIDI synthesizer and having a built-in loop library. More important for classroom use, Mixcraft recordings (like GarageBand projects) can easily be exported as WAV or MP3 files. Figures 5.3 and 5.4 provide a side-by-side comparison of the GarageBand and Mixcraft interfaces.

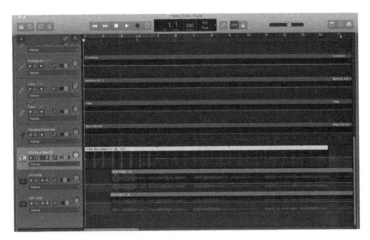

FIGURE 5.3. The GarageBand interface

Audacity

Audacity is a free option for both Mac and Windows. It is an open-source program, which means it was created by a group of collaborators who intended to share their product for free. Audacity is not a "teaser" version of a bigger program (as Finale Notepad is to Finale). Instead, it is a fully featured recording platform available for no cost.

Audacity is a multitrack audio recording and editing program. At its most basic level, it is an easy way to make recordings in a music classroom. It is as simple as pressing the Record button to start recording. Audacity will display waveforms for each track and has a level meter. If the loudest point of the recording lights up the whole level meter, the microphone settings may be too sensitive, and distortion may result. This problem can be addressed by adjusting the microphone level. It should be adjusted so that the loudest point of the recording lights up most of the level meter but not all of it.

Unlike GarageBand and Mixcraft, Audacity is purely a multitrack audio recorder. It does not contain a loop library or allow manipulation of MIDI data. Multitrack recording is helpful for a teacher who is creating a recording one track at a time, as most rock and popular songs are recorded (i.e., recording a drum track, then a bass track, then

FIGURE 5.4. The Mixcraft interface

guitar, and so on), but does not need MIDI capabilities such single-note editing. While this can be useful for some classroom applications, it can be problematic in a rehearsal situation, in which overdubbing multiple "takes" is not desirable. Since it is not a DAW like GarageBand and Mixcraft, Audacity does not have a built-in library of loops, and it is not a MIDI sequencer.

Audacity offers some of the basic functions that a word processor like Microsoft Word does. After highlighting any portion of a recording, the user can cut, copy, and paste that section of the recording. The program offers additional capabilities specific to audio editing, such as adjusting the speed (with and without affecting pitch) and transposing the pitch of the recording. It is also possible to reverse the recording and insert fade in and fade out effects, and to add reverb and many other effects. These capabilities allow teachers and students to edit and control their recordings.

In this program, files are saved with the AUP suffix. It is fine to save AUP files for later use on the same computer; however, it is necessary to export to a different file format before sharing the recording with others. The AUP file does not contain the actual sound clips. Instead, it points to a folder with many little sound clips (approximately one second in length). These little files tend to add up, so it is not practical to share these folders, and when archiving recordings, it makes sense to save the recordings in a more compact file format (such as MP3).

Audacity has multiple export options, including WAV and MP3. When exporting (under the File menu), each format has two options, Export and Export Selection. The Export option will combine all of the tracks in the file into one track and export the entire file as an MP3 or WAV file. The Export Selection option will only mix down the highlighted portion of the file. Through these processes, it is simple to re-create an MP3 or WAV file to share with others, either via a website, email, or file sharing site. In addition, Audacity comes with a fairly extensive menu of automated effects including amplification and fade out, as shown in figure 5.5.

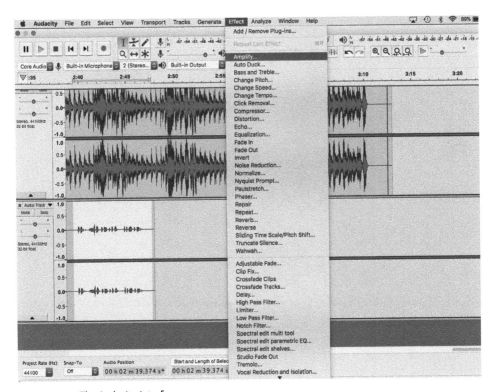

FIGURE 5.5. The Audacity interface

All of the current affordable recording options open new pedagogical possibilities, especially for supporting music learning. The challenge for teachers and students will be to establish the new habits that explore and maximize these opportunities. Some schools are teaching audio recording and podcasting as specific subjects. From a pedagogical standpoint, however, the integration of audio recording, listening, and self-assessment into the routine of music creation, learning, and practice can transform the learning experience.

6

Sequencing Software

Introduction

Music sequencers and digital audio workstations are programs that allow users create, arrange, and manipulate a variety of musical materials. While some of these programs include a standard notation interface, these programs primarily utilize graphic notation systems to assist the users working by ear. These programs have become increasingly robust, able to use MIDI data and import, record, and modify digital audio. The result is that teachers and students now have access to creative tools in the classroom that had been previously reserved for music studios.

Early sequencers were built into hardware synthesizers and drum machines, allowing the user to record and control loops of synthesized sound. As MIDI became the standard information format, allowing music hardware and computers to work together, software synthesizers were developed. This allowed musicians to record the MIDI data from performances on the MIDI-compatible electronic piano keyboard on the computer. Unlike notation programs, software synthesizers have been primarily focused on producing sound, rather than printed notation.

As computers have become more powerful and as more efficient file formats for digital audio have become available, the line between sequencers and DAWs has disappeared. The ability to handle prerecorded sound loops and to record audio has been incorporated into sequencers, which previously had been limited to MIDI data. This merger of sequencers and DAWs has led to programs with greater flexibility to work with high-quality sounds and that do not necessarily require hardware in addition to the computer.

Digital Audio Workstation Functionality

Digital audio workstations generally handle four kinds of data: MIDI data, prerecorded loops, audio recorded by the user, and audio imported by the user. For example, when a choir director plays a piano part into a DAW, the program is recording the specific MIDI data for each individual note for later realization through a software-based synthesizer. Loops are prerecorded repeating patterns that are particularly useful in popular styles of music, since they match the typical patterns used in popular music. When students are browsing through the DAW library looking for a drum groove to match the drumbeat they just picked, they are working with loops. When they are done setting up their bass and drum groove, they might utilize the DAW's recording abilities to record guitar tracks into their song. Finally, users might import a short clip from a familiar song in order to sample a phrase from a favorite artist.

A typical DAW interface is organized in the form of horizontal tracks. Each track represents an instrument or line of sound. The horizontal axis represents the timeline of a piece. A vertical scrubber bar represents what is sounding at any given point and helps the user align multiple tracks. A track can contain any of the types of data discussed, and some DAWs can have a video track as well. Side windows and lower panels that are easily opened and closed allow users to select loops, add audio effects, select instruments, and edit MIDI and audio data. Note the vertical track alignment, loop library, and editing pane of the GarageBand window shown in figure 6.1.

Digital audio workstations offer a wide range of control of sound, allowing users to apply a wide variety of edits to preexisting sounds, including volume, fade in, fade out, trimming, copy, reverb, pan, and transposition. Users cannot modify individual pitches on digital audio tracks, but they can with MIDI tracks. Since MIDI contains performance

FIGURE 6.1. Features of GarageBand

instructions (data) for a synthesizer, users can control pitch, duration, velocity (volume), and timbre. Users can also have global (all track) control over volume and tempo.

When a project is complete within a DAW, users typically have the option to continue saving in the program as a native file or to export it in an audio format. If the project contains only MIDI data, the option to export as MIDI may be present. In general, projects are "mixed down" for export, meaning that the tracks are merged into a single stereo output format. Depending upon the DAW, file formats may include WAV, AIFF, and MP3.

Use in Educational Settings

Digital audio workstations provide a powerful tool for student creativity, in part by offering a wide range of scaffolding. In the same way that physical scaffolding allows an artist to climb safely to paint a mural or ceiling, DAWs provide a foundational structure and knowledge base for learning. For example, a novice musician who many not be proficient at reading standard musical notation can almost immediately begin to make expressive decisions about how to shape musical materials just by using the loop library and intuitive editing tools in a DAW. No prior knowledge of music notation or experience playing musical instruments is required. More advanced users (for example, musicians who play in all of their own tracks) may make more specific musical decisions while a novice might start working with musical loops and sampled recordings. As result, music educators can easily very their instruction to meet their students' level of readiness, and students can immediately begin to make creative decisions without months or years of technical study.

With the immediacy of musical playback made possible by DAWs, even novice musicians can develop auditory and technological acuity. The ease of editing makes musical choices real and reversible via the Undo command. For this reason, artistic decisions are low-risk, allowing great creative freedom. Novice musicians can use embedded tools such as quantization for rhythm correction and transposing features for pitch editing. When working with MIDI tracks, every single note is easily edited via the graphic "piano roll" display.

Entry-Level Software

There are two device-based software programs that stand out in the affordable DAW category: GarageBand and Mixcraft. Both offer easy drag-and-drop creation with loops from included libraries, the ability to import audio, direct recording into the software, and MIDI input using included synthetic instrument sounds. On-screen editing is intuitive, as are features such as volume, pan, and equalizer automation.

GarageBand

GarageBand is a free program that is included on all Apple Macintosh computers. The iOS app version GarageBand is available free from the Apple Store. Its format and capabilities were revolutionary when it was released in 2004, allowing the nonmusician to intuitively work with musical materials and blurring the categories of recording, sequencing, and looping software.

GarageBand comes with a large and often changing library of synthesized instruments and digital loops. These, as one might expect from the title GarageBand, focus primarily, but not exclusively, on timbres and loops found in vernacular music styles. The program can also incorporate still pictures and video in a "movie" track, making it ideal for creating video podcast and multimedia projects. As a part of the iLife suite, GarageBand files can be exported directly to a user's iTunes music library, or files can be saved as MP3, AIFF, WAV, or AAC files.

Mixcraft

Mixcraft is essentially the Windows equivalent of GarageBand. Made by Acoustica, it is not included with the Windows operating system but is available for purchase starting at $49 per computer. It does not run on Mac OS. It offers the same capabilities to users, including the ability to incorporate video, loops, imported audio, recorded audio, and MIDI sequencers. An extensive library of popular music loops, and digital instrument MIDI sounds is included. Like GarageBand, it has an intuitive, track-based interface, as shown in figure 5.4.

Cloud-Based DAWs

Soundtrap, Bandlab, and Soundation are cloud-based DAWs. These online tools allow users to work with limited loop libraries, record their own audio, MIDI, or import both audio and MIDI files for editing and manipulation. All three online DAWs offer limited free versions. Soundtrap and Soundation offer special educational pricing below $5 per student and an even lower per-student cost with a large number of student subscriptions. Both Soundtrap and Soundation also offer LTI functionality, making them popular with schools that use single sign on (SSO) learning management systems (LMSs).

Useful for recording or for creating remixes, user files for cloud-based DAWS are stored by user account (with limits on files sizes) and can be edited and exported. Soundtrap and Bandlab have added collaboration tools that put music production on a par with the collaborative aspects of Google Tools. Soundation includes full-fledged synthesis capabilities. While not as powerful as GarageBand or Mixcraft, these accessible tools are useful for class use and for short-term projects that might not warrant a larger investment. Note the similarity of interfaces, shown in figure 6.2 (Soundtrap), figure 6.3 (Soundation), and figure 6.4 (Bandlab).

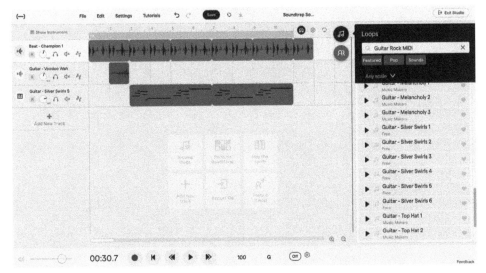

FIGURE 6.2. Basic interface of Soundtrap with loop library

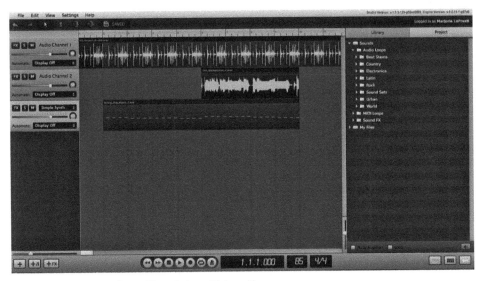

FIGURE 6.3. Basic interface of Soundation with loop library

FIGURE 6.4. Basic interface of Bandlab with loop library

The recent advent of affordable DAWs opened new possibilities in music education, particularly in developing student creativity. In the chapters that follow, the applications of DAWs in a variety of music learning settings will be explored.

7

Loop Libraries and Drum Machines

Tracked and Non-Tracked Software

Looping software allows users to create music using segments of music that repeat. These programs are particularly useful in allowing students to construct (or deconstruct) music in a variety of vernacular styles because these styles are heavily based on repeating patterns. These programs fall into two general categories: tracked and non-tracked. In the first category are programs such as GarageBand, Mixcraft, Soundation, Bandlab, and Soundtrap that use pre-recorded digital audio clips in a track-based format. The second category includes programs that are more "zoomed-in" in that the user works in an interface that controls the rhythm of the individual pitches or sounds in the loops. These programs, such Audiotool, OneMotion, drumbit, O-Generator (shown in figure 7.1), and Groove Pizza generally are not track-based.

As discussed in Chapter 6, looping is just one feature of DAWs such as GarageBand, Mixcraft, Soundation, Bandlab, and Soundtrap. As digital audio workstations, these programs also allow users to record and import their own audio, and all also serve as MIDI sequencers (allowing users to play and record through MIDI keyboards or interfaces).

The non-tracked category contains a variety of interfaces that usually appear as a simulated drum machine, but circular patterns are used in O-Generator and Groove Pizza. What these environments have in common is the user's role in constructing repeating patterns, typically sixteen beats in length. These two programs are cloud-based. Some allow MIDI and audio export in WAV or mp3 formats, while others include MIDI export of the patterns. Though not usually displayed as "tracked," these options generally allow layering in a measure-by-measure process.

FIGURE 7.1. The O-Generator circular interface

Rationale for Loop-Based Software and Drum Machines in Educational Settings

Traditionally trained musicians sometimes view use of looping software as being less legitimate or as cheating because the user does not create the sound and does not make creative decisions at the level of the individual note. Rather than view this as negative, music educators should view looping software as an opportunity to engage students of all backgrounds. Its simplicity is a positive in that it can provide a satisfying entry point and appropriate scaffolding for novice musicians. With a teacher's guidance, the students can learn to make increasingly sophisticated musical decisions. The scaffolding that looping software can provide is only a negative if the students do not grow in their musical understanding.

Having a relatively simple option for creating music provides more tools for the music teacher. By matching a software environment to the students' background, the teacher can furnish a setting that fosters student success. The different structure of various looping programs also offers opportunities to match student' learning styles. The track-based programs, in which students can see the entire song lined up from start to finish, may be a better match for linear thinkers. The non-tracked programs, in which the student views the loop but not the overall piece, or in which the student is making adjustments in real time, may be a better fit for nonlinear or abstract learners. Asking students to reflect on and discuss their experiences with the different formats of such programs may provide insight into students' musical thinking.

Tracked Looping Software

With its focus on pre-existing loops, track-based looping software presents the user with a wider view of a piece of music. In other words, the student is focused on chunks of musical material, rather than zooming in to the details of individual notes. This focus can be useful for addressing the musical concepts of form, texture, and dynamics. In typical performance classes, students are rarely in a position to make individual decisions regarding the form of a piece or how dense or sparse the text of a verse should be. Using track-based looping software, students can begin to explore these concepts with little to no prior training.

For teachers working in this environment, it is important to learn to discern how a work represents a student's musical thinking. This can be a shift in thinking for teachers who are used to evaluating performance. A looped piece is going to be in tune and in tempo and will have the same pitches and rhythms with a good tone each time. Instead, therefore, the teacher must consider the musical decisions that the student made regarding form, dynamics, texture, and selection of loops. Including a student's reflection about his or her creative process as a component of the project can offer insight into those decisions (and can be included in the assessment of a particular process). Via this shift in expectations and attention, teachers can become comfortable in knowing that working with looped materials can be considered a musical effort.

Of course, users of track-based looping programs are not limited to a zoomed-out view. Users are able to "look under the hood" and modify and alter loops. Users are able to alter the tempo and pitch of a loop as well as trim it. If it is a MIDI-based loop, users are able to change the pitch and duration of individual notes. In the case of digital audio loops, users are limited to altering the whole loop. As students become more experienced in working in this environment, the teacher should lead them toward making these types of alterations to serve the students' projects. By offering these capabilities, these programs provide a pathway for students' musical growth, as they learn to make increasingly specific and sophisticated decisions.

Selecting Loops

The process of selecting and placing loops is very similar across programs such as GarageBand, Mixcraft, and the cloud-based options. Each of the programs allows the user to select a series of descriptors to narrow the selection of loops. For example, a user looking for a guitar loop would select Guitar. From there, she might select the adjective Intense

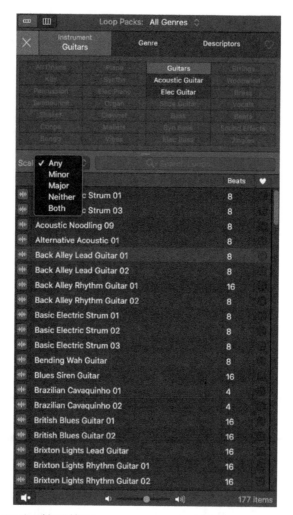

FIGURE 7.2. The GarageBand loop library

to further narrow the selection, as depicted in figure 7.2. The layout and descriptors vary between programs, but the process is essentially the same. Once the number of loops is narrowed, the user can click on the loop in the browser window to preview (hear) the clip.

Placing Loops

Once a user has selected a suitable clip, he can drag that clip onto a particular track (or below a track to add a new track). The clip can then be placed a particular point at the song. By clicking and dragging the middle of the clip, the user can move the clip to a particular location. By clicking the upper right corner of the clip, the user can cause it to be repeated and extended (hence the name *loop*). For example, he might select a one-measure drum pattern and then quickly loop it so that the same pattern repeats for all twelve measures of the chorus.

Matching Loops

A major issue when working with pre-existing loops is matching tempos and tonal content. GarageBand, Mixcraft, and Soundtrap provide a bit of support by automatically matching tempos. Unless the loop shows a time rather than the number of beats, the loop will automatically adjust to the overall tempo of the piece. If users adjust the master tempo, the loops will continue to map to the new tempo. Soundation offers users the option to match the tempo on import or to change (time stretch) at any point during the project.

In terms of tonal content, the loops in GarageBand are generally mapped to the same tonal center, although tonalities vary. If the user changes the tonal center of the piece, new loops will not automatically adjust, but loops that are placed in a track will change if the master tonal center is adjusted. Understanding these processes is important because it affects the level of scaffolding that is provided to students as they work to create in these programs.

Modifying Loops

These programs also vary in the types of modifications users can perform on loops once they have been placed. In all three programs, users can "automate" (or adjust at specific moments in a track) effects such track volume, echo, reverb, and track panning (left and right).

GarageBand and Mixcraft allow for more extensive editing. By opening an editing window, the user can make global and specific changes to a loop. Regardless of whether the loop is MIDI (a software instrument) or digital audio (pre-recorded) loop, the user can modulate the pitch of the whole clip. In the more recent updates of GarageBand (version 6 and later) the user can stretch and move portions of an audio clip without affecting the whole clip. In MIDI clips, the user can edit the pitch and duration of individual notes as well.

Extent of Loop Libraries

GarageBand, Mixcraft, and their online counterparts such as Soundtrap and Bandlab come with libraries of thousands of loops. In GarageBand some loops are not initially loaded in order to save hard drive space, but the user can see the loop in the index and can to download it. A majority of the loops use a single instrument, but some are multitimbral (using more than one instrument). GarageBand and Mixcraft loops tend to be more at the single-instrument building-block level. Users of all programs can record and import their own loops into the library. Additional loop libraries can be purchased or accessed for free online.

Non-Tracked Looping Software

Non-tracked looping programs provide a variety of visual orientations for the user. Some, like drumbit and OneMotion, provide a representation of a loop but not a representation of the whole piece. Others, such as Audiotool, provide a view of the instruments, which are played in real time. By matching these interfaces to students' level of musical experience and learning style, teachers can provide environments with the correct level of freedom to support students' musical learning.

In many school programs, non-tracked looping software is used in conjunction with traditional DAWs that display the loops and other musical material in a linear format. Most programs with a non-track interface provide the ability for users to export their creations as audio or MIDI files. These loops can be imported into most any DAW. Use of both types of looping interfaces can provide students and their teachers the flexibility and scaffolding needed to meet the needs of all learners.

Ableton Live, a more advanced and expensive DAW, provides the ability for users to toggle between tracked "arrangement view" and non-tracked "session view." Ableton's companion website (learningmusic.ableton.com) provides a well-designed sequence of music composition tutorials in drum machine environment. Loops created on the website can then be exported for use in the Live software. This model of web-based tutorial provides scaffolding for inexperienced users and an incentive for users to move on to the more sophisticated Live interface.

Drum Machines

OneMotion Drum Machine

OneMotion https://www.onemotion.com/drum-machine/ is a web page that simulates a basic drum machine. It is typical of most online drum machines. The intuitive interface allows the user to create repeating patterns with up to nine elements of a drum set. The interface shows a nine by sixteen grid, with each of the nine rows representing a timbre and each of the sixteen columns representing a sixteenth-note subdivision of the beat. Each box, which represents the instrument that is sounding, toggles on and off. The user has simple set of play controls for starting, stopping, and jumping to the next screen for a total of two measures. There are global controls for volume, tempo, and echo. The user can also control the overall volume for a specific line (instrument) as well as control the volume (velocity) for each specific note for each instrument. When the user hits Play, the program loops through the selected sounds. The user can make changes while the beat is playing. Options include changing the time signature to two, three, five, six, seven, or eight beats per measure. The 3D button brings up a virtual animated drummer.

The simplicity of this interface can be particularly helpful because it provides a simple visual representation of a drumbeat. Users can intuitively begin to create their own beats in a matter of minutes. Coupled with a listening example, OneMotion can help a user try to re-create the beat from a specific song, which can be a powerful approach to deepening student listening. Figure 7.3 shows OneMotion's 16-column grid that represents one measure of common time in sixteenth note subdivisions, with horizontal rows for each drum sound. This arrangement is typical for drum machines. By

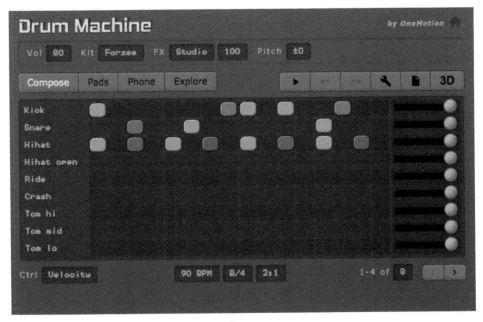

FIGURE 7.3. The OneMotion drum machine interface

switching to the Pads option from the Compose default, the computer keyboard becomes a controller for on-screen drum pads.

Drumbit

Drumbit (https://drumbit.app/) is a free online drum machine much like OneMotion. No login is required, and advertisements appear on screen. Drumbit uses the familiar sixteen-beat grid pattern and has a convenient dropdown menu for changing kit sounds at any time, as shown in figure 7.4. Filters and effects are easily accessed through the main dashboard. A major drawback of drumbit relates to file export or download. Files are saved in a native JSON format rather than MIDI, WAV, or mp3. Drumbit Plus, available for $1.99, is the Chrome plug-in (app) version of the application. Drumbit Plus provides additional kits, effects, and up to 16 patterns (measures). Note that this inexpensive version of the app allows for export of files in WAV format, which is essential for use in educational settings.

Modular Interface

Audiotool

Audiotool.com is a web site that simulates vintage instruments used to create dance beats. Similar to the program Reason, Audiotool provides a virtual table onto which users can drag various drum machines, a bass synthesizer, a tone matrix, and effects pedals and wire them together. Users can manipulate the instruments' dials and sliders just as they

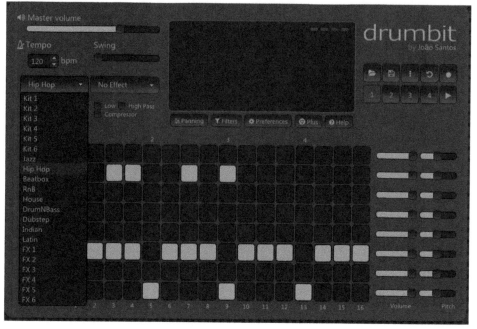

FIGURE 7.4. The drumbit drum machine interface

would if they were playing the original instrument in the 1980s. The result is a very powerful modular interface that allows users to create, perform, and record very complex songs, all for free. This virtual table is shown in Figure 7.5, and includes effects and other tools that can be added to the project by dragging them into place in the main working area of the screen.

Various controls are located around the "table." In the upper left tool window, users can select the cursor and control the view of the table. This is important because in most setups users needs to zoom in to use an instrument, then zoom out when moving to the next piece of equipment. To the right of the table users can select from various pieces of virtual equipment. When they drag a component to the table, they can wire it by clicking one input/output and dragging the virtual wire to another input/output.

At the bottom, users can control the meter and tempo and can also access the Play, Stop, and Record buttons. A pop-up track view is also available from the bottom menu tool bar.

From the top menus, users can save their work (in the cloud on the Audiotool server), export their work to their computer as an mp3 file, and publish their work to the Audiotool web site. This program also allows users to import or record sample sounds and to export the files. The Audiotool environment lends itself both to live performance and to composition because users can control the instruments once the Play button has been tapped, and the Record feature allows users to capture these performances.

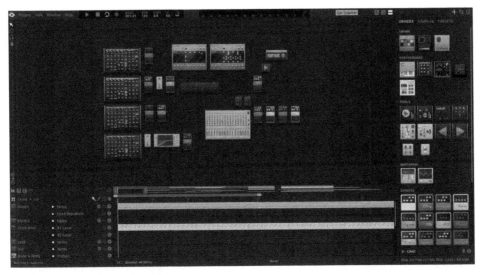

FIGURE 7.5. The Audiotool interface

Audiotool accounts are tied to the users' email addresses, which can be problematic when setting up accounts for student users. It is possible to set up one class account and to allow students to work in parallel on the same account login from different computers. It is also possible to work without a login, but in that case users cannot import samples or save, publish, or export their work. A collaborative feature of the program lets users listen to and add to one another's pieces as well. There are two important caveats for educators: Content posted by other users may not be appropriate for younger students, and collaborating in Audiotool exposes students to a global community of musicians.

This environment is a prime example of the declining costs of technology. The virtual instruments available on this site cost thousands if not tens of thousands of dollars a few decades ago and are now free. All of the original capabilities of these instruments are available, so this site, though powerful, has a significant learning curve. There are supporting tutorial and user sites. This tool is not for use in a quick, one-shot lesson but, rather, is ideal as an environment in which students can immerse themselves and explore music for a longer period of time.

Circular Interfaces

O-Generator

O-Generator (www.o-generator.com) is a sequencing tool that, at first look, is drum machine with a circular interface. The circle represents a measure of common time subdivided into sixteenth notes. Each colored ring is a layer of the texture such as drums, cymbals, toms, bass, and chords. Users can program individual measures and construct elaborate pieces by navigating between measures (bars), as shown in the lower right

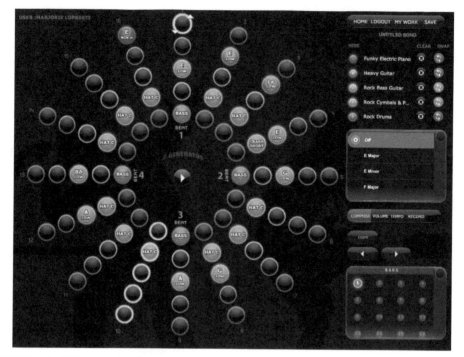

FIGURE 7.6. O-Generator interface

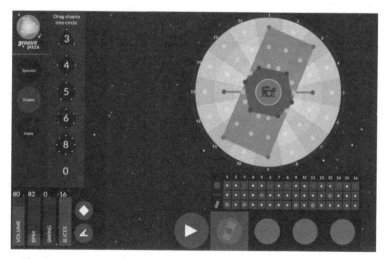

FIGURE 7.7. The Groove Pizza interface showing layers

corner of Figure7.6. This tool provides a structured learning environment that includes carefully sequenced lessons and tutorials, as well as a Create mode. O-Generator offers an app for tablet users as well as a full cloud-based version. Developed in the UK, the program offers user privacy protections that comply with the European Union's General

Data Protection Regulation. School subscriptions are moderately priced and are available as standalone products or as part of the MusicFirst software suite.

Groove Pizza

Groove Pizza is among the applications offered free to schools by New York University's Music Education Lab (https://www.musedlab.org). The circular interface is somewhat similar to that of O-Generator, but layers of music are represented with shapes and angles, creating a virtual layered musical "pizza." The bottom of the user screen provided in Figure 7.7 also shows a grid interface typical of drum machines.

Summary

Looping programs vary widely in design and capability. By removing the need for students to create sound on a note-by-note level, these programs offer new approaches to a wide variety of musical concepts. They also offer a varying level of scaffolding or support for musical novices. Through careful thought about matching student background to software and project design, music educators can make effective and creative use of looping in their teaching.

8

Accompaniment and Practice Software

Software and cloud-based applications have the ability to provide accompaniment and practice support far beyond that of the auditory models of practice tracks and accompaniment frameworks such as Music Minus One. Founded in 1950, Music Minus One, now a division of Hal Leonard, continues to provide high-quality accompaniment backing tracks. Though valuable, this technology has largely been eclipsed in the educational sphere by more flexible programs including Band-in-a-Box, SmartMusic, and PracticeFirst. Apps such as Wurrly offer singers (and potentially instrumentalists) a customizable karaoke-like practice experience with included recording-studio tools. Noteflight notation software also includes a recording option, which enables the notation program to be used as an accompaniment tool. Saved recordings can be submitted as assignments, used to track progress, or used simply for self-assessment.

The ability to easily create an accompaniment for individual or group use is a primary benefit of music technology. In the classroom, computer accompaniments can be used to free the teacher to lead, evaluate, and manage classroom behavior. In the practice room and at home, computer accompaniments can be used to allow students to practice in a helpful and productive context. Not only is this more rewarding for students, but it also allows them to work on playing in tempo and in tune more easily.

A wide variety of programs can be used to create custom accompaniments. Notation programs such as Finale, Noteflight, and Sibelius can be used effectively to create backing tracks, and karaoke-style practice tracks. DAWs and sequencing programs like GarageBand, Mixcraft, and Soundtrap can be used in similar ways. In this chapter the focus is on programs designed to either create accompaniments or easily deliver preexisting accompaniment files to students. Four platforms in particular fall into this category: Wurrly, Band-in-a-Box, SmartMusic, and PracticeFirst.

Accompaniment Software

Wurrly

Wurrly is a highly functional accompaniment and recording online tool and app. Thousands of songs are available that are fully licensed by the company for end users. The team at Wurrly recorded custom backing tracks for each song using full band, guitar, and piano. Users can change tempos and keys in real time and record performances with simple tools. The recording and editing features of Wurrly include some standard audio and video effects and filters. Built-in collaboration features allow users to share their music with friends, with the Wurrly community, or via social media. The primary interface screens for the Wurrly app are shown in figure 8.1.

Band-in-a-Box

First released in 1990 by PG Music, Band-in-a-Box (BIAB) is a long-standing staple of music education technology. The basic version is affordable at $90 and provides powerful capabilities for music educators. The basic purpose of the program is to allow the user to enter a chord progression, select from a wide variety of styles, and then realize that combination in sound. By allowing the user to make decisions at a more general level (i.e., which chords and which style) as opposed to having to enter each note, BIAB can be a time saver for music educators in a variety of settings. Free BIAB apps for iPhone and Android sync well with the desktop version once backing tracks are created, but their functionality for creating new tracks without the desktop version is extremely limited.

The basic version of BIAB comes with hundreds of styles, most focused on jazz and popular music. Several expansion packs with additional styles are available as well. These styles are generally realized in synthesized MIDI sounds, but recently live "real audio" tracks have been added. The user has control over a wide variety of parameters, including tempo, key, muting and timbre of individual instruments and can record via a MIDI keyboard; all of these factors further allow for customized accompaniment. The user is

FIGURE 8.1. The main Wurrly interface screens

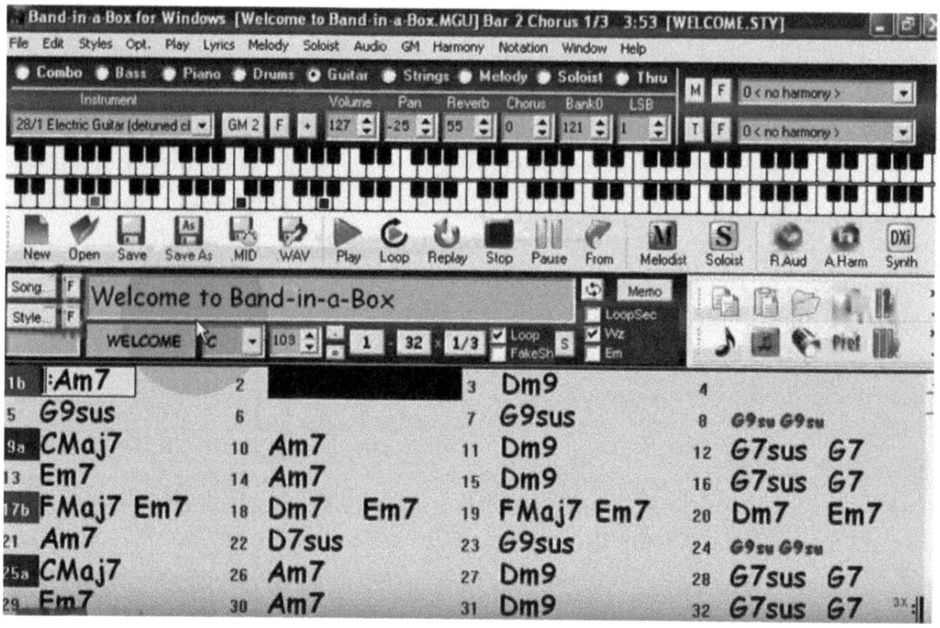

FIGURE 8.2. The Band-in-a-Box default screen

also able to determine the length of the song form and how many times the program will repeat.

The default screen view is the chord chart shown in figure 8.2, but it is possible to view individual instrument parts in standard notation. Once an accompaniment is created, the user can play it in BIAB, export it as a sound file, or export it as a MIDI file for use in another program (such as GarageBand or a notation program). This allows for flexible delivery of the sound file via CD, website, mp3, and so on or as a printed notation.

While the basic features of BIAB have remained unchanged over the years, significant features have been added. A couple of the most impressive include the ability to listen to a recording and fairly accurately discern the chord progression and the ability to create original solos in the styles of famous jazz artists. For example, a user can direct BIAB to the audio file of Miles Davis's famous 1959 recording *All Blues* and learn the changes for *All Blues*. (No big surprise there, but it's a handy feature nonetheless). Then, using these changes (or any other changes), the user can select the Generate and Play a Solo feature in the Soloist menu to have BIAB create an original solo in a specified style, such as that of Miles Davis, over these changes. (Other artist algorithms include Charlie Parker, John Coltrane, Benny Goodman, Pete Fountain, and Herbie Hancock.) These solos are surprisingly recognizable.

For teachers BIAB can be a great time saver because it allows them to create customized, functional accompaniments in short order. For students who are performers, it can be a great practice tool. For less experienced students, BIAB provides helpful scaffolding to allow them to have creative composition experiences.

Practice Software: SmartMusic and PracticeFirst

Whereas Band-in-a-Box allows users to create accompaniments, practice software applications such as SmartMusic and PracticeFirst deliver premade files for users to hear. Students can simply listen and practice along or record themselves and receive detailed feedback about accuracy. Like Band-in-a-Box, SmartMusic has been around since the 1990s. PracticeFirst, powered by Match My Sound, has been available since 2015.

SmartMusic

Introduced as Vivace in 1994,[1] the original SmartMusic system was hardware-based; the user ordered a specific piece of music on a ROM cartridge, which was then plugged into the system. The basic feature which has remained the same is that SmartMusic not only played the accompaniment but could listen to the user and adjust the tempo, or follow the performer as an accompanist would. In current versions of SmartMusic, an audio analysis algorithm listens to and analyzes the performance. Immediate feedback is provided in the form of red (incorrect) or green (accurate) notes. Users and schools pay an annual subscription fee for access to the entire SmartMusic online catalog. The cloud version, shown in figure 8.3, recently became available as a companion (and potential replacement) for the long-standing desktop version.

FIGURE 8.3. Screenshot of the cloud version of SmartMusic

FIGURE 8.4. The colored feedback zones of PracticeFirst

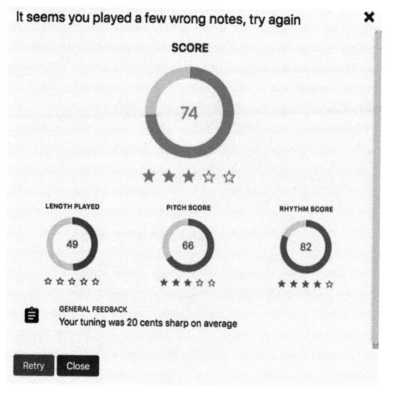

FIGURE 8.5. An example of performance scoring in PracticeFirst

PracticeFirst

PracticeFirst, licensed from Match My Sound by MusicFirst, is similar to SmartMusic in many ways. One primary distinction is that it is exclusively a subscription-based cloudware application. Users select pieces from the library and have the option to practice or perform it with or without accompaniment. A different type of analysis algorithm from that used by SmartMusic provides immediate feedback about pitch and rhythm in the form of green, yellow, and red zones. Users can receive detailed feedback by hovering over the color-coded areas shown in figure 8.4.

PracticeFirst scores performance quality on a percentage basis that also accounts for the length of the total excerpt played. See the score breakout in figure 8.5.

Comparing SmartMusic and PracticeFirst

In both SmartMusic and PracticeFirst, a user starts by browsing the library, selecting a piece or exercise, and accessing the file. In the desktop version of SmartMusic, the file must be downloaded to the user's computer. Some of the files include notation that will appear on the screen, and others do not. The accompaniment sound for method books, exercises, and solos tends to be a synthesized piano or harpsichord, while full ensemble, band, and orchestra accompaniments are digital audio recordings of real ensembles. Regardless of these differences, the user has extensive control over the accompaniment file, including the ability to change the tempo and key. The user can also set up a loop of specific measures, which is useful when practicing a particularly difficult passage.

Each time a user plays the accompaniment, SmartMusic automatically begins to record. PracticeFirst users may listen to the example first and can press Record when ready. Users can then review their performances (a great benefit for students). If students are particularly pleased with their performance, they can send the recording to their teacher directly through the software. Both PracticeFirst and SmartMusic also provide visual feedback about the accuracy of students' pitch and rhythm. After the students have finished playing, SmartMusic displays correct notes in green and incorrect notes in red and shows a summary percentage of correct notes. As stated above, PracticeFirst shows results in green, yellow, and red and scores pitch, rhythm, and duration independently. This feedback should not supplant a teacher's complete assessment of the student's performance but it is very useful, particularly for less experienced students who are still learning to assess their own playing.

Both SmartMusic and PracticeFirst are subscription-based services. SmartMusic's central teacher account is $40 per year, with additional per-student costs of between $4 and $12. The subscription includes online access to the program and to the SmartMusic library. The library's collection includes more than thirty thousand solo and ensemble pieces, and more publishers agree to partner with SmartMusic each year. Initially focused on solo repertoire, the library has expanded to include full band and orchestra pieces, method books, jazz books, vocal repertoire, and aural skills development exercises. PracticeFirst, offered as part of the MusicFirst suite of software, averages $6 per student.

Some repertoire and method books for band, orchestra, and vocal music are included, though pricing for many stand-alone musical scores varies.

Both programs include additional features. Users can easily make mp3 recordings (with or without the accompaniment file), utilize the metronome, and check their pitch with the built-in tuner. SmartMusic also serves as a variable-speed mp3 player. Users can import any mp3 or track from a CD and then speed up or slow down the playback without changing the pitch or the key. This feature is particularly useful when a teacher needs to modify an accompaniment track or when a student is working on a transcription. Both programs also offer teachers the option of adding their own content, exercises, and scores simply by uploading notation files.

With Wurrly, Band-in-a-Box, PracticeFirst, and SmartMusic, teachers have affordable options for providing accompaniments for their students. These accompaniments can support whole-group instruction and enrich individual practice.

Note

1. https://digitalcommons.gardner-webb.edu/cgi/viewcontent.cgi?article=1170&context=education_etd

9

Websites and Learning Management Systems

The Internet has evolved into a platform for user-created content and collaboration. In the field of education, platforms like Google, Weebly, and Wix offer free and inexpensive hosting of websites. Wikis such as Wikidot and PBworks, website platforms intended as collaboration spaces, provide opportunities for teachers, parents, and students to work together to maintain online content. Depending on websites' or wikis' design capabilities, they may be able to host learning tools such as audio practice tracks, links to online resources, embedded video tutorials, and even simple assessments such as quizzes and response forms. Greater collaborative and communication functions continue to be added to free and inexpensive website-building platforms.

In addition, many school districts provide each teacher access to robust learning management systems (LMS). Such systems, which include Blackboard, Moodle, Schoology, Canvas, and Sakai, provide robust communication tools, discussion forums, gradebooks, and the ability for teachers to set up classes and to host and assign lesson material, and for students to upload assignments. MusicFirst provides music-specific learning management software and ready-to-use instructional content including, lessons, quizzes, and full courses. Google, Apple, and Microsoft have entered the education space with student-friendly "domed" environments for schools that mimic many functions of an LMS. These domed environments offer student privacy protections similar to those of LMSs and include a suite of online "office" and design software for general communication, collaboration, and presentation of learning materials.

Systems

Setting clear goals is essential to making good choices concerning website or LMS design and use. Will the teacher use the platform to communicate information to students only or to both parents and students? What types of responses might be needed? Will internal messaging be needed to help prevent a flood of emails? Will the site need to support audio and video? Will it need to allow students to submit items, complete forms, or even contribute content such as new pages? Must the platform support instruction and assessment, too?

Knowing whether two-way communication and shared editing capability are needed is crucial. The next decision regards the extent to which the platform will be used to support or facilitate instruction. Finally, availability of online software may be considered.

Website Features

With almost any website creation, wiki or LMS platform, it is possible to upload and share files of almost any type, from Word files to sound recordings. It is possible to post a Sibelius file and to embed a YouTube video or other video. A basic website can be an efficient way to deliver files to students and can be a central repository of information for a music class, as in the PBworks site shown in figure 9.1. Though the design is simple, the information and navigation tools are clear.

A website designed for a band program might include a PDF file of the band handbook, YouTube videos of performances of the pieces being studied, PDFs of the band warmups and audition materials, mp3 files of recent rehearsal recordings, and fillable rehearsal evaluation forms that the students are to complete as homework. Many webbased tools including Google Forms and Quizmaker facilitate the creation of online quizzes, which can be embedded or linked through websites and wikis.

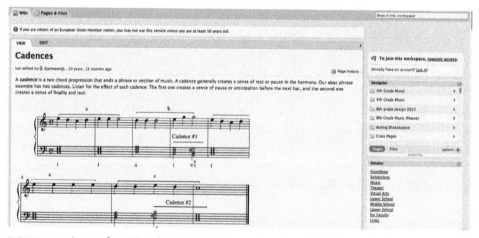

FIGURE 9.1. A page from PBworks (Used with permission from Adele Dinerstein, The Park School of Baltimore)

Instructional websites and wikis, like others, can have multiple pages, linked together. Teachers should consider their educational objectives and build their site accordingly. For example, for a simple one-time project only one page might be necessary. For other settings, more pages might be necessary. A choir director, for instance, might create a page for each work being performed or perhaps a page for each voice part or class section, on which students listen to the rehearsal recordings and share their critiques via file upload or a comment window.

Websites and wikis can be open to the public for viewing or password protected (closed.) Open sites are preferable when the primary goal is communicating with families. Some platforms (such as Wordpress) even allow specific pages to be password protected while primary informational pages are open to all. Teachers, administrators, parents, and students can be given a variety of levels of access from read-only to full site administrator access.

Decisions about differing levels of student reading or editing access depend on the aims of the site. Most platforms, when users are allowed to make changes to the site, make it possible to go back to any stage of a page to view changes and to learn who made them. For example, if a student thought she could just delete a homework assignment from the Homework Assignments page, it would be a simple matter to identify the culprit. Likewise, a high level of editing privileges may be appropriate if a teacher wants to allow students to construct web pages on a shared class site as a place to display their work.

When websites are closed, access to them is restricted, and accounts typically are tied to email addresses. In some wiki platforms it is possible to re-create custom account names and passwords that are not tied to email addresses. This is very helpful, especially when working with younger students who may not have their own email addresses yet. Use of students' official school email addresses is recommended at all times for compliance with COPPA and FERPA laws.

Having a closed site is generally preferable when using the website or wiki for instruction purposes. The restricted access allows students to interact on the site safely and for the teacher to post files, such as rehearsal recordings, that they might not want to post for the general public. Creating a password-protected section of a school website is not always an easy matter and is not a prospect that most school IT support personnel relish. Websites including Google Sites make it possible for individual music teachers to now accomplish this task in a matter of minutes.

Choosing a Platform

Teachers in some situations may be required to use a specific school-sponsored website platform such as Schoolwires (owned by Blackboard) or Google for a public-facing, open webpage. Most, however, have the option to create an additional, more robust website. If the school does not provide access to an online classroom or LMS platform, the choice of a free or inexpensive platform for the music site is a crucial first step.

The functionality of website building platforms varies by provider. Teachers may want to practice setting up a page in various sites to see which feels best to them. A major difference is how the site handles uploaded files. Some sites include the capability to embed files, music, and audio in a specific page, whereas others provide a folder, or virtual hard drive, from which users can link to uploaded files. In either case, the user can easily share word processing files, PDFs, pictures, videos, and, important for music teachers, audio files (mp3 and WAV files).

Website or wiki building platforms are empowering for school music teachers because they provide simple web authoring ability for which they are not reliant on a school's typically limited web resources. This is generally a good thing, but teachers should be aware of the drawbacks, especially before making extensive use of free websites. The teacher's (and possibly students') work is stored on servers outside the school's control. Although the web services providers mentioned in this chapter seem to be flourishing, they are commercial ventures, and there are no guarantees of their continuance. Teachers should be sure that their use of websites and wikis falls within their school's Internet use policy and has the approval of their administrators. Most teachers will, nonetheless, find that the benefits far outweigh any risks and that websites and wikis have great potential for extending and supporting learning of music. The page displayed in figure 9.2 shows a Google site designed for students' work to be posted and shared with others in a membership-restricted forum. Note that the interface is aligned

FIGURE 9.2. Google site with students' work posted

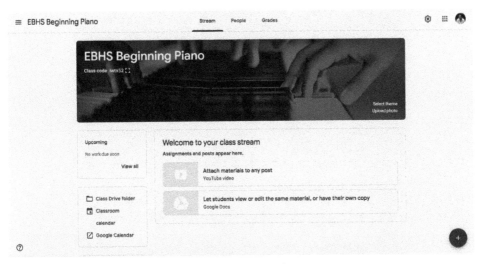

FIGURE 9.3. A sample of the Google Classroom teacher interface

with other Google tools, making it easy for teachers and students to begin using it without formal training.

Online Classrooms

Google, Apple, and Microsoft offer classroom-branded products. As of this writing, these programs are hybrids of integrated online office and design software and communication tools. These "classrooms" are linked web pages presented in a controlled, easy-to-build website, with user-restricted access. Such platforms aspire to the level of LMS, as they provide the ability to enroll student users (and teachers) in specific classes, or sets of web pages. Almost universally, access to such platforms must be school-sponsored, and student access is tied to a school-sponsored email address. Files are stored in linked online drives, not specifically in a dedicated classroom storage server. Teacher materials and student work are shared, linked, or embedded using these separate drives. Some online music software companies such as Noteflight and Soundtrap are providing the ability to link to these online classrooms via LTI (Learning Tool Interoperability), so that software-based activities appear as assignments in the student's task list. Figure 9.3 illustrates the basic teacher interface for Google Classroom.

Learning Management Systems

Learning management systems bear many similarities to multipage instructional websites and online classrooms. As a rule, access to the LMS is granted with user credentials. Depending on the age of the students and the specific LMS, student email addresses may be needed. Teachers can post instructional information and media including photos, audio and video. Most LMSs include file uploading, embedding, and linking capability

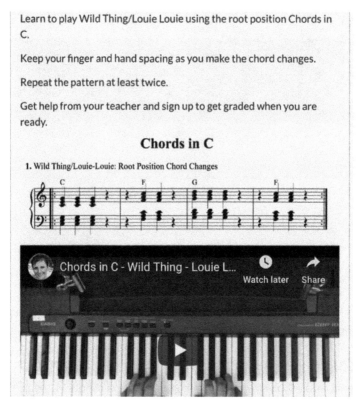

Learn to play Wild Thing/Louie Louie using the root position Chords in C.

Keep your finger and hand spacing as you make the chord changes.

Repeat the pattern at least twice.

Get help from your teacher and sign up to get graded when you are ready.

FIGURE 9.4. A page from the Canvas learning management system

with simple editing tools. Teachers post lessons, as well as create assignments for students that may include student responses, discussion forums, or file uploads of work created offline or in other applications. Figure 9.4 displays a student lesson in the Canvas LMS with printed notation inserted as an image, along with a tutorial video.

What makes an LMS far greater than a website or wiki is its specific, protected file storage and its arrangement of users into classes, with permissions as students, teachers, and even instructional aides. Assignments and assessments are hosted directly on the LMS, with project submission or upload just one click away in order for students to post to a secure environment. Robust communication tools, messaging, and discussion forums are included. All of the ease of page creation and editing from websites, wikis, and online classrooms is present in an LMS. A proper LMS also includes lesson planning and gradebook functions. Many LMSs include integrated software using LTI protocols, such as Noteflight or Flipgrid, a popular video-based discussion forum.

Many schools provide free access to LMSs, easing the path to enrolling students in classes. Some LMSs, such as Schoology and Edmodo, were designed primarily for K–12 schools and provide parent access. Blackboard, Moodle, Canvas, and Sakai are used extensively at the high school and college levels. MusicFirst, a full LMS with integrated music software and an extensive library of courses, units, lessons, and assessment tools,

FIGURE 9.5. MusicFirst program choices

provides the most robust option for music education. Its currently available software is shown in figure 9.5. Costs for MusicFirst begin at $2 per student, so this option skirts the edge of affordability for many schools.

For each music teacher, selecting the best and most cost-efficient option is a uniquely personal choice based on many factors. Table 9.1 provides a snapshot of the content and communication hosting options discussed in this chapter to help with the decisionmaking process.

TABLE 9.1 Commonly used LMS, class, website, and wiki options

Learning Management Systems	Educational Level	Ease of Use/Accessibility
Blackboard	High school/college	Some learning tools integrate easily; little music-specific content
Canvas	High school/college	Some learning tools integrate easily; little music-specific content; available lessons are not actively approved or curated
Sakai	High school/college	Some learning tools integrate easily; little music-specific content
Moodle	Middle school/high school	Some learning tools integrate easily; little music-specific content
Schoology	Middle school/high school	Some learning tools integrate easily; little music-specific content
MusicFirst	Upper elementary through college	Includes carefully designed and curated music lessons and curricula; can include integrated software like Noteflight and Soundation
MusicFirst Junior	Pre-K to 5	Includes carefully designed and curated music lessons, songs, and curricula; includes age-appropriate software
Classroom Platforms	**Cost/Grade Level**	**Ease of Use/Accessibility**
Google Classroom	School district subscription required/Elementary through high school	Some learning tools integrate easily; little music-specific content
ClassDojo	Free; premium features available for subscription fee/Elementary school	Teacher content sharing platform included Parent communication features included
Edmodo	Free/Elementary through high school	Teacher content sharing platform included Parent communication features included
Public-Facing Websites	**Cost**	**Ease of Use/Accessibility**
Schoolwires (from Blackboard)	School subscription only	Editing is very awkward
Google sites	School subscription only	Editing is intuitive, but formatting is very limited
Weebly	Free; premium options available for purchase starting at $5/month	Editing is intuitive; formatting options are excellent
Wix	Free; premium options available starting at $13/month	Editing is intuitive; formatting options are excellent
Squarespace	Starts at $12/month	Editing is intuitive, formatting options are excellent
Wikis	**Cost**	**Ease of Use/Accessibility**
Wikidot	Free version very limited; pro versions start at $50/year	Editing is intuitive; free version is enough for a basic website
PBworks EDUHub	Free for up to 2GB storage; upgrade to 40GB and more security features, $109/year	Editing is intuitive; file management is very good

10

Videoconferencing

Videoconferencing opens up a world of possibilities as music teachers can interact with other teachers and classes regardless of distance. This is a timely development as funds and resources for field trips and for clinicians and guest artists diminish. Interactions that would otherwise be impossible owing to travel, cost, or both are now easily possible. Whether it consists of an elementary general music classroom having a "penpal" concert with students on another continent, having a mentor or composer give your band a clinic from three states away, or private teachers giving lessons to students in remote areas without other opportunities for music lessons, videoconferencing offers exciting opportunities.

This strategy has been in use in educational settings for decades. The new and important change is that rather than requiring a dedicated classroom with expensive equipment, free videoconferencing is now possible between any two computers that are online and have a camera. In order to use this technology, teachers need to consider which software to select, secure a camera (if one is not built into the computer), and set up the conference in the classroom, which for larger classes will include an LCD projector. All of the options presented here also function via mobile apps, though the small screen size makes that method less than optimal for classroom use.

Free Videoconferencing Options

The most prominent software choices for videoconferencing include Skype, Google, Facebook, and Facetime. All of these applications are free and are cross-platform (not limited to a specific operating system). Each requires setting up an account and creating a user name. So-called freemium options like Zoom.us, GoToMeeting, and Whereby.com (previously operating as Appear.in) offer limited usage for free, with powerful features and connectivity available to paid subscribers.

Skype

Perhaps the most common platform for videoconferencing is Skype. Created as an Internet-based phone service, Skype allows users to communicate via text message, voice, and video between computers for free. Users can also call traditional telephones. In addition, Skype users can send files to each other during a chat and share views of their screens. Skype is integrated into the Microsoft 365 suite, allowing for collaboration in online word processing, spreadsheet, and presentation software.

As a standalone application Skype is a downloadable program and mobile app (available at www.skype.com). Once the program is downloaded, the user sets up an account and user name. The program allows users to search for other Skype users and to maintain a list of contacts. When connected, the user can display different statuses (allowing other users to know whether it is all right to call or not). Calling another user is as simple as clicking the text, phone, or video camera icon. In the Skype Preferences menu (under Audio/Video), the user is able to independently select which camera and which microphone input to use on a call. This is helpful because in many instances the optimal placement of the video camera, computer, and microphone may differ depending on classroom setup.

Google Hangouts

Google's Hangouts video chat service can be a web browser (Mac and PC) or a standalone program (PC only). When users have established a Google ID, they have the option of placing the Chat module in their Google page. Through this module users can add contacts with whom they can text, use voice chat, or use video chat. As with Skype, users have control of which cameras and microphones are used. As a component of the Google suite, users can collaborate on Docs, Slides, and other applications during the videoconference.

Facebook

Facebook offers video chat through the Chat function on the user's Facebook page. This platform offers fewer controls on audio and video input than do others, but it might be convenient for teachers who are already familiar with Facebook. It is important to separate personal and professional online personas; teachers should consider carefully whether they want to have their personal Facebook page open in front of students. Although it is possible to switch between being logged in with your personal screen name and as the administrator of a group or forum, the chat function is only enabled when you are logged into a page (not a group or forum). In other words, Facebook user John Doe, who is also the administrator of the Acme High School Band page, would only be able to have a videoconference while logged in as John Doe, not while logged in as the administrator of the school band page. Though not optimal for classroom use, Facebook may be more accessible than other platforms for some users, and it points to a trend of video interactions becoming increasingly ubiquitous in software programs.

Facetime

Facetime is a videoconferencing app built into the operating system of all Apple computers, phones, and tablets. By using cell phone numbers, email addresses, or Apple IDs, users can text, talk, or share video. The lack of cross-platform functionality is an obvious drawback, but the interface does work well for Apple users, and it offers multi-user videoconferences without additional charges.

Freemium Subscription Options

Additional web conference providers offer the ability to host sessions and invite multiple attendees. Whereby.com and Zoom.us offer basic online meeting hosting with video for free, with limits to session length and number of participants, depending on the platform. Free and low-cost options such as a basic GoToMeeting subscription ($18/month) also limit the ability to record sessions and set a cap on the number of free attendees. Schools with Google accounts may benefit from checking on the availability of Google Hangouts to host meetings. The option to add many participants is limited to Google Enterprise subscribers. The plethora of emerging web-based meeting platforms is ever-changing, as are pricing options.

Hardware: Webcams and Projectors

Built-in cameras are now standard on many desktops and laptops. In some instances, this camera is more than adequate. When a built-in camera is not available, or in situations where the camera needs to be detached from the monitor, affordable webcams are easily available and can quickly make any computer a video conferencing station. Prices for webcams have dropped to the point where even cameras in the range of $30 to $40 have sufficient resolution and frame rates to provide adequate streaming video.

There are practical matters to consider when purchasing a webcam. The first is picturing where the camera needs to be placed in the classroom. Can it be clipped to the computer? Will it need its own stand, or can you devise your own stand? How far will the camera be from the computer, and do you need an extension for the USB cord? Do you have another microphone, or do you need a built-in microphone in the webcam? While there are many more high-end features in more expensive cameras, addressing these basic questions allows teachers to easily stream good-quality video from their classroom.

The final component of a videoconferencing system is a projector. When conducting a videoconference with more than a few students in the classroom, a projector will also be necessary, so that all of the students can readily see the screen. Many classrooms already have projectors mounted in the room, and most schools have portable projectors available, so this component should not add to the music teacher's cost of videoconferencing.

Classroom and Rehearsal Applications

Although Internet-based videoconferencing dramatically opens the possibilities for bringing the world into a music classroom, there are some limitations to consider as well. The primary drawback is the issue of lag. The process of compressing and transmitting video and audio information does take time, so there is a lag between the actual production of sound and its presentation at a remote location. This lag is small enough that it does not hinder normal conversation, but it does prohibit accurate joint performance of music. The compression process also lessens the audio quality of the transmission. For high quality concert presentations, professional organizations turn to premium transmission services, but unfortunately access to premium services like Cisco Telepresence or Tenveo video conferencing equipment in K-12 schools is virtually impossible. Going forward, it is reasonable to expect that the quality will improve and lag time will decrease for free and inexpensive options. The current state of technology is more than adequate to provide excellent musical experiences for students that would not have been possible otherwise.

A few factors should be considered when setting up the videoconference in the classroom. Ideally, a practice videoconference should be conducted before doing this for the first time. If music is going to be performed as part of the conference (as presumably it would be on at least one end), the microphone (probably built into the computer) should be placed at an appropriate distance from the performers, and gain levels should be adjusted in order that a strong audio signal is achieved without distortion.

Just as a director would consider where a guest clinician or audience would be seated when visiting, the camera should be placed with the same considerations of the visitor's view. An additional consideration is the placement of the screen and projector so that the students in the room may see the remote visitors. If the students are going to be interacting directly with the visitors, it is helpful to align the camera and screen so that the students can look into the camera while viewing the remote screen. (Otherwise it can be awkward when the students feel they are addressing the visitors while appearing to the remote viewer to be looking elsewhere.) Figure 10.1 shows a typical setup with students in ensemble seating, the web conference projected for students, and the microphone and webcam-computer placed near the typical podium location. Figure 10.2 shows the projector image from a meeting with the composer via web conference. Note the placement of the laptop and projector near the podium.

Before conducting the videoconference, it is advisable to test the setup and to check with the school's IT person regarding any issues with the school's firewall and bandwidth settings. Keep in mind that demands on the school's Internet connection vary at different

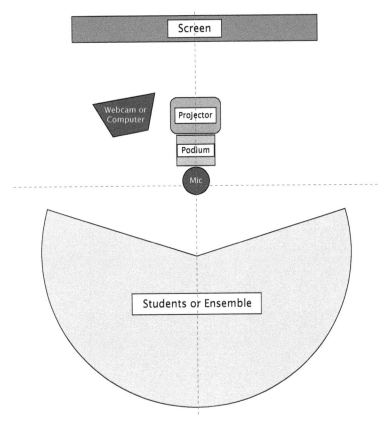

FIGURE 10.1. Web conference setup diagram

FIGURE 10.2. SCHSBANDS_Twitter image used with permission from Lauren Staniszewski, Stoney Creek High School, Rochester Hills, MI.

times of the day and that conducting a videoconference during a time of high demand can lead to interruptions in the audio or video stream. Also, some schools block the ports used by some videoconference software. If that turns out to be the case, possible solutions include trying a different application (for example, if iChat's port is blocked, Skype's port might be open) or requesting that the IT person open that port during your videoconferences.

Possible applications of Internet-based videoconferencing in the music classroom are wide and varied. With travel eliminated as a barrier, many new kinds of interactions have become possible. From private lessons to remote clinics, from exchange concerts to real-time collaboration, the travel costs are reduced to zero. Application of these possibilities are included in a sample lesson plan for middle or high school orchestra, provided in Chapter 13.

11

Online Resources, Media, and Collaboration Tools

Online resources provide a wealth of content and functionality for everyone, not just music teachers. In the vastness of the Internet, no single list of resources could ever be comprehensive or remain fully up to date. For this reason, this chapter focuses on free, reliable resources that have proved useful to many music educators and that are likely to continue to function into the future. Many of these tools are discussed in other chapters, with attention to classroom applications. Each offers a free version, and many offer enhanced subscription versions that typically offer more features or are free of advertising.

Social media options will not be covered in depth here. Social media use has been under scrutiny in many schools, as the platforms designed for adults generally do not have sufficient privacy controls for use in public schools. As a rule, services such as Twitter, Instagram, and Facebook do not readily provide the type of recordkeeping for school communications necessary to be in compliance with Freedom of Information (FOIA) and Open Public Records Acts (OPRA). Many teachers find social media to be a valuable, effective means for keeping in touch with families and promoting the wonderful things happening in their programs. Refer to your school's policy regarding use of social media for school-related activities.

Use of social media for professional development and networking is highly recommended. Many virtual professional learning networks (PLNs) thrive on Facebook, and regularly scheduled topic-specific conversations, or "tweet-ups," occur on Twitter. Peer-to-peer platforms including Pinterest and Teachers Pay Teachers are of great value for those looking for new ideas, but fall outside the scope of this discussion.

The following tables are included for comparison of similar technology tools, and to aid in the exploration and decision-making process.

General Technology Tools

Productivity Tools	Function and Description	Cost
Microsoft Office Suite	Word processing, presentations, spreadsheets, forms, collaboration/sharing, cloud storage Desktop, cloud, mobile apps and synchronized blended versions available with Office 365 Very robust editing and formatting tools Integrates with many LMSs	Free basic version; full version free for most teachers
Google Tools	Word processing, presentations, spreadsheets, forms/ quizzes, collaboration/sharing, cloud storage, website builder Cloud-based, with optional mobile apps Backup and sync function for automated desktop computer storage redundancy available Somewhat limited editing and formatting tools Integrates with Google Classroom and many LMSs	Free basic version; full version free for many teachers
Dropbox	Cloud storage and file sharing	Free and enhanced paid versions

Music and Media Tools

Media Streaming and Storage	Function and Description	Cost
Google Photos	Cloud storage and sharing for photos Integrates nicely with other Google tools	Free
Imgur	Cloud storage and sharing for photos and video Social media tools and user self-promotion features Tools include GIF and meme generators	Free basic account; full version about $3/ month
Flickr	Cloud storage and file sharing for photos and video 1,000 free photos/videos Pro version with unlimited storage, no ads, and rapid desktop upload Includes access to external apps and custom tools through API (application programming interface).	Free basic account; pro version $6/month
YouTube	Video and music streaming, sharing, and storage Free versions are adequate for most educators to access content uploaded by others and to post content for students. Simple video editing tools included. Premium accounts used primarily by businesses Most content is moderated; parental controls and school filters are quite effective in making the space safe for students	Free; free account to upload; premium account $12/month
Vimeo	Video streaming, sharing, and storage Useful for storage and embeds to custom websites since making videos hidden from natural search is very simple Fewer content controls than YouTube, likely not a tool for younger students Fabulous for hosting and embedding teacher-created content.	Free; Vimeo Plus costs $7 per month with additional pro versions up to $75/ month

Media Streaming and Storage	Function and Description	Cost
Spotify	Music streaming Limited free version includes ads, playlists, and search function Premium version allows the compilation of unlimited playlists, which can be shared, including with embed code for interactive playback in another website or LMS	Free with ads; from $99/year or $10/month includes unlimited playlists
Pandora	Music streaming Limited free version with ads Basic premise uses model of genre-specific "stations" Paid versions remove ads and include custom "stations" and search functions	Free with ads and ability to skip songs; from $5/month to remove ads, $10/month to search and create custom playlists
Google Play Music	Music storage and streaming Free version allows users to stream free music with ads and play music the user uploaded free from ads Paid subscriptions include YouTube Music, are free from ads, and offer additional customization features Includes YouTube Music	Free with ads; from $10/month to remove ads and add custom playlists
Amazon Music	Music streaming with playlists and stations Search by artist or title Voice control with Alexa-enabled devices	From $8/month
Apple Music	Music streaming with playlists and stations Search by artist or title Voice control with Siri	From $5/month

Videoconferencing Tools

Videoconferencing	Function and Description	Cost
Skype	Free videoconferencing Premium version included in many schools' Microsoft Office subscriptions Premium versions allow more participants and access from landlines	Free; premium versions start at $5/month
Zoom	Free videoconferencing for meetings of up to 40 minutes Schedule meetings in advance and record meetings Pro plans include more participants, Skype interoperability, and LTI integration for use in LMSs	Free; pro versions start at $15/month
Whereby.com (formerly Appear.in)	Free videoconferencing Very easy to use Up to 4 attendees in a virtual "meeting room" that retains the same web address for each use Rooms can be "locked" when not in use Pro plans offer more users, rooms, attendees, controls, and scheduling tools	Free; pro versions start at $10/month
Google Hangouts	Free videoconferencing for up to 10 people Free group chats for up to 150 people Limited presenter controls Free Chrome browser plug-in	Free

Social Media and Collaboration Tools

Social Media and Professional Collaboration	Function and Description	Cost
Twitter	Messaging platform Used by many educators to share information with students and parents Many educational professional learning networks (PLNs) use hashtags (#) to group messages, share news, and pass along articles about education trends Some PLNs have recurring "tweet-ups"—scheduled conferences	Free
Instagram	Photo and video messaging and social networking platform. Owned by Facebook, so accounts are easily linked. Popular features include photo and video filters for special effects, geotags and geofilters for location, and hashtags for topics of interest, as with Twitter.	Free
Facebook	Social networking Many educational "Groups" collaborate here "Music Teachers," "I Teach Music Technology," and "AP Music Teachers" act as professional sharing and problem-solving communities Use of Facebook with students and parents is not recommended by most schools	Free
LinkedIn	Professional networking Online profile and networking platform Used to some extent to share research and news Popular among job seekers Use of LinkedIn with students and parents is not recommended by most schools	Free; premium version starts at $30/month
Remind	Teacher-student messaging. Targeted to teachers and school groups for contacting students and parents to share information by text message, through the free app, or online. Students and parents "subscribe" to teachers' classes, so it is an opt-in system. May not be compliant with Open Public Records Act (OPRA) requirements in public schools.	Free

Discussion Forums and Quiz Tools

Discussion and Collaboration Tools	Function and Description	Cost
Padlet	Discussion forum organized like sticky notes Easily moderated by the teacher	Free
Mentimeter	Polling with options including bar graphs and word clouds	Free
Flipgrid	Video discussion forum Students respond to prompts from the teacher and can respond to one another through recorded webcam video	Free

Quiz Makers/Games	Function and Description	Cost
Kahoot	Multiple-choice game that students can join from any device Many free, premade games available for music All game questions can be edited, and new game questions created easily Intense music and sound effects	Free
Quizziz	Similar to Kahoot without the music and sound effects	Free
Plickers	No student tech devices required Students orient cards with unique QR code–like shapes to answer multiple choice-questions	Free

Libraries of Musical Scores and Recordings

Musical Scores and Recordings	Function and Description	Cost
IMSLP	International Music Score Library Project https://imslp.org/ Vast library of public domain music in PDF, MIDI, XML, notation file, and audio formats Functions like Wikipedia, with user-uploaded and verified content	Free; donations accepted
CPDL	Choral Public Domain Library http://www2.cpdl.org Library of public domain choral music in PDF, MIDI, XML, notation file, and audio formats Functions like Wikipedia, with user-uploaded and verified content	Free; donations accepted
Band Music PDF Library	https://www.bandmusicpdf.org/ Library of public domain band music in PDF format Specialties include sharing missing parts for scores and corrections to parts containing errors	Free; donations accepted
Classical Archives	https://www.classicalarchives.com/ Library of music from all eras in MIDI and audio formats Many excellent recordings available	Limited free membership; subscriptions start at $8/month or $80/year
MuseScore.com	Community of MuseScore software users who post to the MuseScore database Scores are available to members for download as PDF, XML, and MuseScore files	Free

Music Theory and General Knowledge Resources

Music Theory and General Knowledge	Function and Description	Cost
musictheory.net	Comprehensive music theory lessons and exercises for beginning through advanced students Ear training including intervals, chords, scales, and pitch identification Customizable exercises for teachers, including verification codes for teacher use after students complete exercises	Free online version; mobile apps for $3 and $4

Music Theory and General Knowledge	Function and Description	Cost
teoria.com	Detailed and challenging music theory lessons suited to intermediate and advanced students English and Spanish languages Robust ear training including melodic and harmonic dictation	Free; subscription for teachers to enroll students
musicca.com	Music dictionary, theory lessons, and exercises including ear training with excellent, reliable content Developed in Denmark; some English usage and syntax is awkward, but does not compromise validity or functionality	Free
dolmetsch.com	Comprehensive music dictionary and encyclopedia Interface feels out-of-date, but content is impressive	Free
Wikipedia	Love it or hate it, it's where students go first Most music-related articles are valid and correct, but may not be readable for elementary and intermediate students	Free; donations accepted
Music Map	https://musicmap.info Visual, interactive explanation of relationships among musical genres and subgenres, particularly for popular music	Free

Online Music Production

Music Production	Function and Description	Cost
Ableton Learning Music	https://learningmusic.ableton.com Carefully sequenced lessons in beat, melody, bassline, and chord construction using a grid interface for note entry and real-world examples Student product can be exported in Ableton format	Free
Ableton Learning Synths	https://learningsynths.ableton.com Click and drag graphical interface for exploring and learning the fundamentals of synthesis and common synthesizer controls	Free
Drum machines	Too many to include here; see Chapter 7	
DAWs	See Chapter 6	

Teaching Resources for Popular Music

Popular Music Resources	Function and Description	Cost
Teach Rock	https://teachrock.org/ Full curriculum and lessons backed by Steven Van Zandt and designed by educators with music, arts integration, and STEAM standards alignment	Free; donations accepted
Little Kids Rock	https://www.littlekidsrock.org/educators-free-resources/ Resources for starting and running Modern Band program in schools (guitars, bass, drums, vocals) Teachers apply for grant funding, supported by NAMM and music industry sponsors	Free; resources available; donations accepted

Popular Music Resources	Function and Description	Cost
Shed the Music	https://www.shedthemusic.com/ Lessons in scales, chords, and ear training Premium courses in music production and mixing	Free; subscriptions start at $50/year for individuals and $400/year for one teacher with unlimited students

Teaching Resources for Elementary and General Music

Elementary and General Music	Function and Description	Cost
Beth's Notes	https://www.bethsnotesplus.com Comprehensive index of songs for elementary music with detailed sort functions including regions, subject matter, and musical content Games, lesson plans, and Orff arrangements available for purchase (included for subscribers)	Free access to song search; subscription $13/month or $129/year
Mama Lisa's World	https://www.mamalisa.com Songs and rhymes from around the world, searchable by geographic origin, language, or type of song Includes streaming audio, video, and sheet music for many songs	Free; Online store to purchase books
Incredibox	https://www.incredibox.com Interactive website and app for creating and mixing by adding articles of clothing and accessories to animated beatboxers Rhythm, melody, and harmony layers are intuitive Paid app users can download final mixes as audio files	Limited free online version; apps for mobile devices and desktop computers starting at $4
Isle of Tune	http://isleoftune.com Child-friendly graphical sequencer in which users design a community with roads, houses, trees, streetlights, and so on As car drives around, music plays	Limited free online version; apps for mobile devices starting at $4
Chrome Music Lab	https://musiclab.chromeexperiments.com/ Music learning and creation tools with graphical interfaces including beat maker, melody maker, and song maker Song maker allows export as MIDI and WAV files Interactive audio learning tools about waveform, pitch, harmonics, and arpeggios	Free

12

Technology for General Music

General music is a broad discipline that includes elementary music classes, as well as many forms of middle school and high school music cycle and elective courses that are not primarily performing ensembles. Many parallels exist across grade levels and across the varied topics and activities covered in this broad range of classes. Likewise, the many differences in instructional needs makes it prudent to consider the needs of elementary general-vocal classes first, then expand to include strategies for middle and high school students.

At their core, all school music classes likely will make use of general educational technology tools such as

- Online classroom managers like Google Classroom, Schoology, Socrative, or ClassDojo (or a full LMS like Moodle, Blackboard, or Canvas)
- Presentation tools such as PowerPoint, Sway, Google Slides, Prezi, or Keynote
- Projection systems and interactive white boards
- Note-taking and -sharing tools such as Google Docs, OneNote, and Evernote
- Surveys and information-gathering tools like Google Forms or SurveyMonkey
- Quiz tools including Plickers, Kahoot, Google Quizzes, and Quizzizz
- Online collaboration, communication, and file sharing with Google and Microsoft tools, Dropbox, Flipgrid, and Seesaw
- Communication tools including email, Remind, and even Twitter.

Elementary Music Classes

Typical activities in elementary music classes pre-K to approximately fifth grade include singing and playing classroom instruments such as recorder, pitched percussion or Orff instruments like xylophones, and rhythm percussion. For recorder, many online and software-based applications can facilitate student learning. Practice and assessment technologies outlined in previous chapters (SmartMusic, PracticeFirst) work well with recorder. A plethora of YouTube videos provide tutorials and practice tips.

With a simple DAW or recording program (GarageBand, Audacity), teachers can support student learning by capturing recordings or creating practice tracks. The recording feature in Noteflight Classroom is a low-cost, integrated music reading and recording practice platform that is age-appropriate for students as young as seven or eight years of age.

Most elementary music classes revolve around singing together, often with movement or games. Programs such as The Singing Classroom provide song tutorials complete with movement and game instructions, song sheets, and videos for singing and playing along. This is primarily a tool for the teacher for preparation and for whole-class use, priced at approximately $150 per year.

Platforms such as MusicFirst Junior and Quaver provide full curricula, lesson plans, some interactive software, and an engaging student interface. MusicFirst Junior also provides login access for every student at school or at home, much like an LMS. Students can complete assigned tasks or explore and create with age-appropriate software including Morton Subotnick's Music Academy and Groovy (a DAW for children). MusicFirst Junior includes a multimedia music encyclopedia and falls within most school budgets at approximately $399 per year for the entire school.

Many elementary music classes include "centers." Students rotate among activities, some of which are completed independently, and some of which include group or teacher-guided experiences. Many music educators structure centers using iPad apps such as GarageBand or use free web tools including Incredibox, Isle of Tune, and Chrome Music Lab. Basic notation programs such as Noteflight and Finale Notepad fit into the rotation of centers, with students notating familiar melodies and rhythms or creating music using teacher-supplied "note banks." Games such as StaffWars and free resources at www.musictechteacher.com help gamify music learning and practice in whole-class and centers-based activities.

Technology-facilitated performance is increasing in elementary programs, as well as in upper grades. Electronic instruments including touchpad synthesizers and plethora of virtual instruments for tablets and mobile devices like the iPad bring electronic music making into reach. Apps provide immediacy by giving users the ability to manipulate sound with a swipe of the screen or by tapping a few keys—no special training, instrument rentals, or lessons required. Many such apps provide accessibility features that would be helpful to students with physical or neurological learning challenges. The virtual instruments in the GarageBand app provide an excellent starting point, as do some of the tools in the Chrome Music Lab online apps. The list of mobile apps for music is vast;

a helpful starting place for classroom-tested websites and apps for elementary music is maintained by Amy Burns at http://amymburns.com.

Communication with parents is central to daily life in a vibrant elementary school program. Use of simplified LMS-like platforms including Google Classroom, ClassDojo, and Seesaw is particularly helpful in the elementary music setting. ClassDojo functions as a class management and record keeping tool that also allows photos and videos to be shared with parents. Seesaw is a student-driven portfolio platform in which students take ownership of sharing photos, audio, and video with their families. Both ClassDojo and Seesaw require paid subscriptions for approximately $120 per year.

Middle and High School Music

Many middle and highs school cycle classes and electives have a technology focus. Increasingly, schools are integrating music creation and composition with DAWs as well as with notation programs. In addition, classes at this grade level often include guitar, ukulele, and piano instruction. Online resources and practice software can help keep students engaged while allowing for the differentiated pace many students need. As in elementary music, some middle school classes include a rotation or alternation model with guitar performance, piano practice, and DAW-based music creation.

Technology for Music Theory

Technology can facilitate music theory learning and practice at all grade levels. Free web-based tools and gamelike exercises are available at http://musictheory.net, http://teoria.com, and http://musicca.com. Free tools can cause scheduling and tracking challenges for class assignments, but the content is excellent. Robust software including Essentials of Music Theory, Practica Musica, Ear Master, Breezin' Thru Theory, Musition, and Auralia all provide in-depth theory training and classroom controls but may be cost-prohibitive for most schools. Audio Timeliner, a free software program available at http://www.singanewsong.org/audiotimeliner/, provides the function of adding annotations to an audio recording. This feature may be helpful for students and teachers alike to create markers and callouts relevant to formal or harmonic analysis. In addition, every music theory course can make use of notation software. Refer to Chapter 4 for notation software options.

Sample Lesson Models
Elementary General Music

Grade 3	ABA Form with *The Nutcracker*
	Lesson to occur over 2–3 class meetings
Objectives	Students will be able to respond to and represent ABA form through movement.
	Students will be able to create a composition in ABA form using classroom instruments, with contrasting rhythms and dynamics.
	Students will be able to create a composition in ABA form using Groovy Music (or other age-appropriate loop-based software) with contrasting melodies, rhythms, and textures.
Key Vocabulary	ABA = ternary
	Melody
	Rhythm
	Dynamics
	Texture
	Timbre (optional/advanced)
Materials	Recording of "March" from *The Nutcracker* by Tchaikovsky
	Variety of classroom instruments, including pitched and unpitched percussion, and recorders if available
	Devices for students to use software (tablets, Chromebooks, computers)
Whole Group Instruction/ Activity	1. With entire class, listen to "March" from *The Nutcracker*. Instruct students to listen carefully for opening melody, then raise both hands ("goal") when the melody returns.
	2. Engage students in detecting and notating the meter (2) and rhythmic motive of the opening melody. Develop (or look online for) a movement activity to match the opening A section. Pantomime a sword fight with the Mouse King during the B section.
	3. Lead student to draw the connection—ABA or ternary form?
	4. Ask student to think about why B seems busier. [Is it faster? (no) What's going on?] Introduce the idea of *texture*.
	5. Encourage students to think of any other music they know well that is in ABA or ternary form.
Student Task 1	(Optional: divide class if not enough devices or instruments are available—some students work on Task 1 while others work on Task 2)
	1. In groups of 2 and 3, have students use classroom instruments to create a *short* composition in ABA form. Tell students:
	a. Use contrasting rhythms and dynamics to make the A and B sections different.
	b. Write down some notes to yourselves if needed.
	c. Practice your composition.
	d. Be sure about how you will begin and end your performance.
	2. Allow a minimum of 10 minutes prep and practice time.
	3. Facilitate student performances.
	4. Complete evaluation of compositions with rubric during the class performance if possible.
Student Task 2	1. In groups of 2–3 students or solo, use Groovy Music (or alternate software or website) to create a short piece in ABA form.
	a. Use contrasting timbres (instrument sounds), melodies, and rhythms to make the A and B sections different.
	b. Think about changing the *texture* in the B section.
	c. Listen carefully as you finish each section and modify your music to make sure it flows.
	d. Trade devices with a classmate to check for ABA form and help with ideas for improvement.
	2. Instruct students how to save work in progress and when complete
	3. Facilitate student listening session to hear compositions.
	4. Complete evaluation of compositions with rubric during the class listening session if possible.

Grade 3	ABA Form with *The Nutcracker*
	Lesson to occur over 2–3 class meetings
Evaluation	Formative:
	In-class performance of movement while listening to "March"
	In-progress assessment of student compositions
	Summative:
	Rubric-based evaluation of acoustic and technology-based compositions

Grade 3 Student Composition Score Sheet	Possible Points	Points Earned
Represents ABA form clearly	10	
0 = no discernible B section		
1–3 A and B present, but no return of full A section		
4–6 ABA discernible, but little change for B		
7–9 ABA clear, with 2–3 changes for B		
10 ABA clear, many changes for B		
Delivery	10	
0 = No performance or file provided		
1–3 Starting/stopping during performance/playback		
4–7 One or two glitches in performance/playback		
8–10 Smooth, confident performance/playback		
Classwork	10	
0 = Did no work		
1–3 Contributed a little to the project		
4–6 Contributed about half the time		
7–9 Contributed most of the time		
10 Worked consistently the whole time		

Middle School General Music

Grade 7	Variations on a Theme
	Lesson to occur over 3–5 class meetings
Objectives	Students will be able to identify theme and variations in listening examples.
	Students will be able to describe musical attributes that contribute to interesting variations.
	Students will be able to present a piece in theme and variations form using multimedia/presentation tools.
	Students will be able to create variations on a familiar theme by performing on an instrument or singing, and using DAW software such as GarageBand or Soundtrap.
Key Vocabulary	Theme and variations form
	Meter
	Timbre/instrumentation
	Key/mode
	Tempo
	Dynamics
	Articulation
	Texture
Materials	Recordings of *Variations on America* by Charles Ives and *American Salute* by Morton Gould
	Supplemental recordings in theme and variations form
	Devices for student use including software
	Headphones

Grade 7	Variations on a Theme
	Lesson to occur over 3–5 class meetings

Whole Group Instruction/ Activity 1 Discussion Forum	(Students will need devices to log into shared document or discussion forum.) 1. With entire class, listen to the Ives. While listening, take notes in a shared document (Google Doc) or discussion forum, noticing the musical features of each variation. Pause the recording between variations to allow time for students to collaborate on their responses to the variation. 2. Listen to the whole piece again, asking students to listen more deeply for elements such as texture, key/mode, and articulation, and add to their notes. 3. Invite students to describe the generic structure of theme and variations (starts with the "plain theme," etc.)
Whole Group Instruction/ Activity 2 Written Response	(Students will need devices to log into a personal document or Google Form to be turned in.) 1. With the whole class, listen to the Gould. Have students document and submit a written assignment about what they hear, and compare the Gould to the musical content and structure used by Ives. (Teacher option: Ask for a written narrative or complete a teacher-prepared questionnaire like a Google Form.) 2. After listening, instruct students to turn and pair-share with a classmate. 3. Gauge the class—students may want or need another listening to complete the writing task.

Student Task 1 Presentation (to be completed during or outside of class time)	(Students will need devices with Internet access and a presentation tool like Slides, Powerpoint, or Sway, Internet access, and headphones.)
	Option—students can work individually or in pairs
	1. Instruct students to search online for 5 minutes to locate and select a different theme and variations composition. Once selected, they *must* alert the teacher. Only 1 use of a given piece allowed. No one else in the class may select the same composition.
	*Start a list on the board or shared forum so students can see classmates' selections.
	2. Instruct students to create a presentation with one page or slide for each section of their selected theme and variations pieces.
	  a. Title section/slide must contain the title of the piece and composer.
	  b. Each subsequent slide should correspond to a section of the piece and contain key words about the music in that section.
	  c. Sync the music to slide/page transitions.
	3. Students will submit projects electronically.
	4. Students will collaboratively develop a grading rubric.
	5. Teacher—create a Google Form or other tool as a live rubric so students can evaluate their peers' projects.

Student Task 2 Composition	(Students will need devices with access to a DAW or notation program and headphones.) Option—students can work individually or in pairs. 1. Instruct students to select a simple tune that they can play or sing, as they will need to record that as the theme for variations. (Suggestion—for students with limited experience, teach "Hot Cross Buns.") 2. Use the DAW software to record the theme. 3. Add at least 3 variations, each in a different tempo (if the software allows tempo changes), different rhythmic feel, instrumentation, and so on. 4. Students will submit projects electronically. 5. Students will collaboratively develop a grading rubric. 6. Teacher—create a Google Form or other tool as a live rubric so students can evaluate their peers' projects.
Evaluation	Formative: Individual engagement and contribution to shared document/discussions while listening In-progress assessment of student compositions Summative: Rubric-based evaluation of acoustic and technology-based compositions

Suggested Score Sheet in Llieu of Collaboratively Created Rubrics	Possible Points	Points Earned
Discussion responses to Ives, *Variations on America* 0 = No submission 1–3 1 minimal/basic contribution 4–6 1 detailed contribution 7–9 2 acceptable contributions 10 2 or more detailed contributions	10	
Written responses to Gould, *American Salute* and comparison to Ives, *Variations on America* 0 = No submission 1–3 Basic information 4–7 Good detail 8–10 Excellent detail and insight	10	
Theme & variations presentation 0 = No submission 1–3 One or two slides with minimal information (incomplete) 4–6 Slides for most or all sections of piece with minimal information 7–9 Slides for each section of piece with most information 10 Excellent detail and insight, including slide design/graphics that fit each variation	10	
Theme & variations composition 0 = No submission 1–2 Basic recording of theme and attempt at one variation 4–6 Theme plus 2–3 variations with a few musical variables per section 7–9= Theme plus 3 variations with 2–3 musical variables per section 10 Theme plus 3 or more variations with notable musical quality including 3 or more musical variables per section	10	

Middle or High School Music Technology

Grade 9–12	Creating a Song Cover
Objectives	Students will be able to define *cover* as a new recording of a preexisting work. Students will be able to perform the main melody of a song on a MIDI instrument into a DAW. Students will be able to flesh out the recording by adding percussion tracks and harmony. Students will be able to apply basic engineering effects including volume controls, pan, and EQ to create a pleasant, balanced final product. *Note: This lesson assumes that students already have rudimentary skill recording with MIDI and audio inputs, setting up microphones, and basic editing within a DAW.
Key Vocabulary	Cover DAW Fades Pan EQ
Materials	MIDI input devices (keyboards, pads, MIDI guitar and/or drum interfaces) Devices for student use including DAW software and access to a shared document or discussion forum Headphones Optional—teacher-prepared form for student song selection and production plan

Grade 9–12	Creating a Song Cover
Whole Group Instruction/ Activity 1 Discussion Forum	1. Introduce examples of song covers; include time for class discussion/ brainstorming of song covers that are familiar to students. Beware of tendency for students to including sampling and remixing. The entire song should be represented to qualify as a cover. 2. Encourage students to explore https://secondhandsongs.com/. 3. Each student must post 1 song cover to the discussion forum *not* already added by another student. Include title, cover artist, and earliest original artist (if available).
Whole Group Instruction/ Activity 2 Song brainstorming Affinity pairing Song production plan	1. Group discussion question: What songs can *you* perform? Include melody and chords/bass line. Singing *does* count as performing. 2. Facilitate student formation of pairs and trios based on musical affinity and abilities. 3. Each group will choose 1 song to record. 4. Develop a written plan: who is recording melody, harmony, other tracks of the song. (All students will have permission to use loops. Editing and engineering tasks such as level balancing, pan, and EQ to be completed collaboratively.) 5. Submit written plan as a shared document or using teacher-prepared song production form.
Student Task 1 Recording (to be completed during or outside of class time)	Option—students can work individually at teacher discretion. 1. Rehearse with electronic and/or acoustic instruments. 2. Create "1st take" scratch tracks to test equipment, set microphone levels, help establish tempo (set the metronome) and basis for legit percussion and harmony tracks. 3. Capture a clean recording of the melody/lead. 4. Edit and rerecord as needed. 5. Listen through headphones and room speakers to finalize adjustments to track volume levels, pan, EQ, and other effects.
Student Task 2 Peer Feedback	1. Students will submit projects electronically in MP3 format to shared location (Microsoft Teams). 2. Students will listen to at least 2 other projects and offer constructive feedback for improvement. 3. Students will edit/rerecord own projects to work toward completion. 4. Students will submit finalized projects electronically in MP3 format to shared location. 5. Students will collaboratively develop a grading rubric. 6. Teacher—create a form or other tool as a fillable rubric so students can evaluate their peers' projects.
Evaluation	Formative: Individual engagement and contribution to shared document/discussions In-progress assessment of student work while recording, giving feedback, and adjusting based on feedback Summative: Rubric-based evaluation of project(s)

Suggested Score Sheet in Lieu of Collaboratively Created Rubrics	Possible Points	Points Earned
Discussion responses to covers/ https://secondhandsongs.com/ 0 = No submission 1–3 1 minimal/basic contribution 4–6 1 detailed contribution 7–9 2 acceptable contributions 10 2 or more detailed contributions	10	

Suggested Score Sheet in Lieu of Collaboratively Created Rubrics	Possible Points	Points Earned
Written song production plan 0 = No submission 1–3 Basic information 4–7 Good detail—basic steps and assignments of "who's doing what" 8–10 Excellent detail and clear path to completion	10	
Song Cover 0 = No submission 1–5 Submission barely represents the selected song 6–9 Fair representation of melody and one additional layer 10–14 Fair representation of melody, harmony, percussion tracks 15–18 Good representation of melody, harmony, percussion tracks with some attention to engineering 19–20 Exemplary musicianship and production	20	
Peer Feedback 0 = No submission 1–2 Responded minimally to one project 4–6 Gave partial response to two projects 7–9 Responded to two or more projects and incorporated at least 1 suggestion into project 10 Gave astute and meaningful responses two 2 or more projects and incorporated at least 1 suggestion into project	10	

Middle/High School Music Theory

Grade 9–12	Composing with Parallel and Contrasting Phrases
Objective	Students will be able to compose a 16- or 32-measure original composition in AABA form with parallel phrases in AA, and a contrasting phrase in B. *Note: This lesson assumes that students already have fundamental skill entering notes into the notation program of choice.
Key Vocabulary	Parallel period Contrasting period Tonic Dominant
Materials	Devices for student use including notation software Headphones Optional—MIDI input devices

Whole Group Instruction/ Activity 1 Finish the melody	1. Preliminary instruction—parallel and contrasting periods (examples: Foster's "O Susanna," Bach's "Minuet in G," Schumann's "Wild Rider," http://www.teoria.com/en/tutorials/forms/phrases/04-parallel.php, http://www.teoria.com/en/tutorials/forms/phrases/05-contrasting.php)
	2. Take additional examples from theory textbook, teacher library, or student suggestions.
	3. Individually, students will complete two musical examples (see figures 12.1 and 12.2):
	  a. Finish the given phrase to create a parallel period.
	  b. Create a contrasting period by composing another but different phrase that ends on the tonic.

Grade 9–12   **Composing with Parallel and Contrasting Phrases**

Parallel Period Construction

Phrase 1 (implied half-cadence)

Phrase 2 - complete this phrase using the same rhythm as Phrase 1, but with an impied authenic cadence

Contrasting Period Construction

Phrase 1 (implied half-cadence)

Phrase 2 (implied authentic cadence, with significant differences in melody and rhythm)

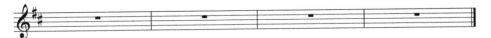

Student Task 1 Composition (to be completed during or outside of class time)	1. Using notation software, compose an opening *singable* melody in your choice of key and time signature. Decide if this melody will work best as a 4-measure or 8-measure phrase. End the phrase on a pitch that signals the *dominant* harmony. 2. Repeat the same phrase beginning and modify the ending to land on the *tonic*. 3. Create a contrasting phrase that fits the same musical universe. Options include reversing melodic direction or modifying the melodic or rhythmic motive. 4. Repeat the second phrase.
Student Task 2 Peer Feedback	1. Students will share notation files with peers or set up a "gallery walk" during which students will rotate among their classmates devices to check out their work. 2. Using a discussion forum, shared document, or comment feature in the notation software, students will leave feedback for classmates, verifying phrase and period construction. Comments should include attention to melodic and rhythmic elements in addition to cadences.
Optional Student Task 3 Animated Music	1. Using examples above from teoria.com, as model starting points, use screen capture, presentation, and/or video production software to create a music video that illustrates the musical structure. 2. Include or choose colors and images to enhance the music. 3. Seek feedback from at least two classmates. Include the names of these classmates in credits during final frames. 4. Share or post the final video.
Evaluation	Formative: Individual engagement and contribution to shared document/discussions In-progress assessment of student work while recording, giving feedback, and adjusting based on feedback Summative: Rubric-based evaluation of project

Suggested Score Sheet in Lieu of Collaboratively Created rubrics	Possible Points	Points Earned
Finish the melody 0 = No submission 1–3 Minimal submission; no completed musical periods 4–7 1 partially completed musical period 8–10 1 completed musical period 11–14 1 period completed, 1 partially complete 15–18 2 completed musical periods with rudimentary compositional skill 19–20 2 completed musical periods with distinguished compositional skill	20	
AABA Composition 0 = No submission 1–3 Partial submission, no complete phrases 4–7 Complete opening A phrase 8–10 Complete AA parallel period 11–13 AA plus partial contrasting B 14–16 AA plus complete contrasting B ending on dominant 18–20 AABA form with parallel and contrasting periods	20	
Peer Feedback 0 = No submission 1–2 Responded minimally to one project 4–6 Partially responded to two projects 7–9 Responded to two or more projects and incorporated at least 1 suggestion into project 10 Gave astute and meaningful responses two 2 or more projects and incorporated at least 1 suggestion into project	10	
Optional Video 0 = No submission 1–4 Submission barely represents the AABA form and period construction 5–8 Fair representation of melody and AABA form and period construction with images 9–10 Exemplary musicianship and production	10	

13

Technology for Performers and Ensembles

Band, choir, and orchestra classes often are larger than other classes in the school. While they have specific music instruction needs, teachers need to streamline as much of the recordkeeping for these students as possible. Technology can play a big role in maximizing rehearsal time. Much of the technology used to support group music learning is applicable in the private lesson or studio setting.

As with general music classes, middle and high school ensemble classes can use many general educational technology tools. These include

- LMSs like Moodle, Blackboard, or Canvas, or a less robust tool like Google Classroom, Schoology, Edmodo, or ClassDojo
- Presentation tools such as Powerpoint, Sway, Google Slides, Prezi, or Keynote. While these tools may not be used for direct instruction, as in general music they can provide a simple way to post daily activities, rehearsal plans, and general announcements. In such electronic forms, sharing with parents online and keeping records is simplified.
- Projectors, interactive whiteboards, and document cameras to project musical scores and magnify fine motor skills like fingering and bow technique.
- Surveys and information-gathering tools like Google Forms or SurveyMonkey
- Quiz tools including Plickers, Kahoot, Google Quizzes, and Quizzizz
- Communication tools including email, open-access websites, apps like Remind, and careful use of social media such as Twitter, Instagram, and Facebook
- Spreadsheets and databases for managing music libraries and inventories of instruments and uniforms

Software for Ensemble Classes

Notation Software and Score Readers

Teachers and students alike will need access to notation software to create arrangements and custom compositions including etudes. Online libraries including IMSLP and CPDL hold vast quantities of public domain music in MIDI format. Notation software is needed to render these MIDI files playable. Refer to Chapter 4 for a detailed discussion of notation software options. Much music is also available in PDF format. Programs like Playscore, MuseScore, and Photoscore can render sheet music images into usable, editable, playable music notation. ForScore is by far the most widely used music reader and annotation tool for mobile devices. This paid app is available for iOS only, so adoption in school settings has been somewhat limited.

Recording Software

Whether for use during class or for independent student use, recording software is indispensable. With simple audio or video recorders on cellphones or quality microphones and recording software, every ensemble director can track student progress with a portfolio of recordings. For both teacher and students, careful, reflective listening often helps develop plans to achieve meaningful musical growth. Audio editing software such as Audacity may be needed for preparing audition materials and creating archival recordings. Such DAWs as GarageBand, Mixcraft, Logic, and ProTools are needed for creating practice and accompaniment tracks.

Practice and Accompaniment Software

Excellent results can be achieved using a simple record-along strategy with practice tracks in a DAW or notation in Noteflight. Wurrly, designed originally for singers, provides high-quality backing tracks and an in-app recording studio with instant transposition and tempo controls. If the budget allows, a subscription to a practice tool with real-time assessment like SmartMusic or PracticeFirst will greatly enhance the practice experience. Chapter 8 provides a detailed discussion of practice and accompaniment software alternatives.

Sight Reading Software

Competition-bound ensembles need to practice sight reading regularly. Currently, only one software platform, Sight Reading Factory, autogenerates unique sight-reading examples. Other options for sight reading practice include using LMSs or projection systems to share sight reading examples drawn from online public domain libraries.

Sample Lesson Models

Though articulated for specific disciplines and age groups, these lesson models are easily adaptable by changing the type of ensemble or the specific hardware or software used to achieve the desired learning and musical outcomes. They are intended solely as frameworks to be customized and fleshed out into full lessons to meet the needs of the students enrolled.

Elementary or Middle School Band

Elementary Band	Eighth Note Reading and Performing
Objective	Students will be able to read and play melodic and rhythmic examples with eighth notes.
Key Vocabulary	Sixteenth notes Sight reading
Materials	Central class display (projector, smartboard, document camera) "Nottingham Castle" by Larry Daehn (Manhattan Beach/GIA Publications)
Whole Group Instruction/ Activity 1	1. Review eighth notes with method book examples. Practice counting and playing. 2. Project Sight Reading Factory examples—rhythm only with half, quarter, and eighth notes. Practice at least 3 examples with whole ensemble playing concert B♭ or concert E♭.
Whole Group Instruction/ Activity 2	1. Pass out music for "Nottingham Castle." 2. Use projection system or document camera to display the score. Allow students a few moments to look over their own parts and look at the conductor's score starting at measure 19. If this is the first time students are seeing a conductor's score, explain the arrangement of parts. 3. Identify the eighth-note patterns at measure 19. Which instruments play eighth notes? Count the rhythms aloud. Then play the rhythm on each instrument's starting note at measure 19. 4. What other kind of rhythm patterns are present? 5. Allow students 2 minutes to work through their own notes mm. 19–28. Rehearse the whole section as written.
Student Task 1	(may be completed in school or at home) Use Sight Reading Factory to complete assigned sight reading task that includes eighth notes in a rhythm-only example.
Student Task 2	(may be completed in school or at home) Use Sight Reading Factory to complete assigned sight reading task that includes eighth notes in a melodic example with conjunct motion only.
Evaluation	Formative: In-class performance of eighth notes Summative: Rubric-based evaluation of individual sight-reading examples (10 points per example: 1 point for each accurate measure in 8 measures, 1 point for tone, 1 point for musicianship and phrasing)

Intermediate School Choir

Choir	Breath Support and Long Phrases
Objective	Students will be able to breathe appropriately to sustain and energize long phrases.
Key Vocabulary	Breath support Articulation
Materials	Central class display (projector, smartboard, document camera) "The Water Is Wide," arr. by Audrey Snyder (Hal Leonard)—SSA, SAB or SATB as needed for voices in choir
Whole Group Instruction/ Activity 1	1. Lead or have students lead physical warm-ups, stretching. 2. Lead breathing warm-ups on low, slow breath, exhaling on *s* with hand gesture to show how much breath is left (8 beats, 12, 16, 20, and so on). 3. Lead vocal warm ups on 5-note scale with sustained note at end (8, 12 or 16 beats). 4. Demonstrate and have students add gesture/movement to sustained tone to activate energy into tone quality. 5. Direct students to remove/stop performing gesture but keep energy in sustained tone.

Whole Group Instruction/ Activity 2	1. Listen to a recording of a performance of the piece online. Discuss as a class or in small group:
	  a. What do you notice?
	  b. What challenges might our choir face in learning this piece?
	2. Sing the opening phrase, all singers in unison. Direct students to:
	  a. Add a gesture to activate the sustained tones.
	  b. Identify places where a breath might be wanted but is musically inappropriate.
	  c. Identify places to breathe.
	  d. Reinforce energy/activation of sustained tones.
	  e. Locate words and phrase ends that need very clear articulation of consonants.
	3. As lessons progress, switch from all singers on melody to harmony parts as written. Insist on sustained, activated tone from all singers.
	4. If all students have a device, create recordings in which all sing together, but each student holds a device to capture his or her individual singing prominently. (This creates in-class reference recording to help with the student task below.)

Student Task	(may be completed in school or at home) Instruct students: 1. Record and submit your "day 1" recording of yourself singing the opening section of the piece. 2. Write a short reflection on how you plan to improve your breath support, energetic singing, and articulation to communicate the music.
Evaluation	Formative: In-class performance Summative: Rubric-based evaluation of individual recorded examples (10 points per example: 5 points for a complete recording with attempt at active sustained tone, 5 points for a sincere reflective statement)

Middle or High School Orchestra

Orchestra	Expression and Composer's Intent
Objective	Students will be able to examine the musical score for expressive marks and interact with the composer to gain insight into composer's intent.
Key Vocabulary	Dynamics Articulation Phrasing
Materials	Central class display (projector, smartboard, document camera) *Orion and the Scorpion* by Soon Hee Newbold, available from FJH Music Publishing, Inc. External webcam External microphone Prearranged video conference with Soon Hee Newbold
Whole Group Instruction/ Activity 1	1. Instruct students to look through their scores, and notice places with expressive markings. Encourage students to think about the composer's intent in placing them. 2. Establish a Padlet or another online discussion tool add notes with specific measure numbers for places where dramatic expressive markings are present in student parts. Instruct students to post questions about any places in the music where they think an expressive marking might be desired, but was not indicated by the composer.
Whole Group Instruction/ Activity 2	1. The teacher will establish a video link with Soon Hee Newbold. Allow her access to the class Padlet. 2. Invite the composer to engage students in an introduction. 3. Ask the composer to respond to student questions. 4. Perform the piece for the composer. 5. Solicit detailed feedback and suggestions. 6. If feasible (depending on latency), allow the composer to conduct or correct a few sections of the work.
Student Task	(may be completed in school or at home) Instruct students to use Flipgrid or another online forum to post reactions to meeting the composer. Students should respond to these questions in their electronic submissions: 1. What did you learn? 2. Did anything surprise you? If so, what? 3. Describe in musical terms and playing technique how you will integrate the composer's feedback and suggestions.
Evaluation	Formative: In-class performance and interactions Summative: Rubric-based evaluation of online reflection (30 points: 10 points for each question posed in Flipgrid/online discussion)

Private or Small-Group Lesson (in Person)

Voice Lesson	Italian Diction
Objective	Students will be able to articulate text of "El Grillo" with correct pronunciation and accurate rhythm.
Key Vocabulary	Articulation Elision
Materials	Score for "El Grillo" by Josquin des Prez, printed or electronic (public domain) Recording device such as tablet, phone, or computer with Audacity or a DAW

Voice Lesson	Italian Diction
Instruction/ Activity 1	1. Lead warm-ups (of teacher's choice) to work on diction, including tongue twisters. 2. Play an exemplar recording of "El Grillo" while assisting students in following the score. 3. Encourage student(s) to identify places where the text seems tricky. 4. Work with student(s) to speak the text in rhythm. Work on forward placement of *l* sound in "grillo." 5. Help student(s) notice vowel elisions—two words with vowels that blend together on one note. 6. Rehearse each section at slower tempo to emphasize diction.
Instruction/ Activity 2	1. Record a practice track at reduced tempo of the student's part with teacher accompaniment (using a notation-file playback of all parts). 2. Listen to this practice track critically. Ask the student to help identify areas need correction before it is used for independent practice. 3. Rerecord as needed for a "clean take" at reduced tempo.
Student Task	(may be completed in school or at home) Instruct student to: 1. Use PracticeFirst or Noteflight to practice with other voice parts, but with student's voice part muted. 2. Gradually increase to performance tempo, carefully checking each recording for accurate and clear diction. 3. Submit the final version to the teacher electronically.
Evaluation	Formative: Student performance and progress Summative: Rubric-based evaluation of submitted recording (20 points: 10 points for accurate pitches and rhythms; 10 points for diction)

Private or small group lesson (remote)

Piano Lesson	F Major Scale and Chord Changes
Objective	Students will be able to play a 2-octave F Major scale and primary chords in root position and with inversions.
Key Vocabulary	
Materials	Teacher-provided musical score (via website or LMS) Computers or devices with Internet access and videoconferencing platform External webcams or movable cameras
Instruction/ Activity 1	1. Teacher (T) asks Student (S) to play C Major scale, 2 octaves. 2. T displays F Major scale via screen share and asks S to identify differences. 3. Presence of B♭ necessitates change of fingering for right hand. T moves camera to capture right hand and demonstrates. 4. S moves camera and repeats for teacher. 5. T demonstrates two-octave F Major scale with both hands, noting that both thumbs play on C. 6. S repeats scale for teacher. 7. T screen records or shares completed video of F Major scale with student for review and aid during practice.

Piano Lesson	F Major Scale and Chord Changes
Instruction/ Activity 2	1. Process above is repeated with primary chords in F: F–B♭–F–C7–F. 2. T displays notation. 3. T performs chords in root position and with inversions for student, noting that B♭ and C7 both require the "black key" B♭. 4. S moves camera and repeats for teacher. 5. T screen records or shares completed video of chord changes with student for review and aid during practice.
Student Tasks	Instruct student to complete these tasks independently: 1. Practice F Major scale with metronome or online metronome app. 2. Practice F Major chord changes. 3. Record and upload both exercises to LMS or teacher website. 4. Select a song in the key of F Major and begin practicing for next lesson.
Evaluation	Formative: Student performance and progress during videoconference Summative: Rubric-based evaluation of video performance (20 points: 10 points for scale; 10 points for chord changes)

14

Technology in Your Music Classroom

This book began with generic terms about technology in the music classroom. Now, it is up to you to decide how to use technology in *your* music classroom. The task of each educator, on a daily basis, is to choose wisely if, how, and when to integrate technology into each lesson. The resources are vast. Some of the gear and software is shiny and exciting. Nevertheless, pedagogical choices should guide the use of technology. Place music learning and creative outcomes first in your priorities. For technology use outside of moments spent teaching, seek the best tools to save time and energy on routine tasks. This will provide more time for music making. For students, choose the most appropriate technology to facilitate learning, streamline assessment, support creativity, maintain communication, and aid in differentiated instruction.

Anchor Points Revisited

The three anchor points presented at the beginning of this text serve as a guide to best-practices for integrating technology into music education.

By keeping *student learning first*, educators set priorities for learning based on musical objectives. They seek pedagogies and technologies that will best achieve those objectives while meeting the needs of students, and providing appropriate differentiation and scaffolding. This anchor point reinforces the general educational technology framework of TPACK—aligning the technology, pedagogy and content knowledge in context of student needs.

When music educators use *just enough technology to get the job done*, the focus remains centered on music learning and creation. Most every technology has engaging elements that can distract from musical objectives. With greater use of technology in music class, the opportunity for distractions and technological glitches increases.

By remembering that *"you do music, students do technology,"* teachers retain their primary role as music expert and learning guide. Barbara Freedman expounds on Dave Williams's work with the axiom "Teach music. The technology follows." In her classroom practice, she praises and rewards students for teaching her and fellow students new software functions and shortcuts. Students can and do assume the role of technology expert on occasion. Such shared responsibility fosters a culture of collaboration and mutual respect.

Getting Started

One aspect of music education that will not change is the critically important role of the music teacher in facilitating music learning. As powerful technological tools become available and affordable, it is still the teacher who must find the best ways to utilize the tools to support student learning. This requires a teacher to try something new. With all of the competing demands placed on teachers, maintaining a focus on implementing technology-based teaching strategies requires a commitment to exploring change. However, this change can be kept manageable by focusing on one aspect of technology at time. There is no need to try every technology or idea in this book (in fact, that would probably be ill advised). Instead, a wiser approach is to try one or two ideas, refine the strategy to fit your needs, and when it has become a regular aspect of instruction, try another strategy. While this book presents starting places that are affordable, there are certainly other wonderful opportunities provided by more expensive technologies. For teachers seeking such equipment, the most effective advocacy for investment in music technology is to show students working with it. The strategies provided in this book provide a good starting point toward that end as well.

Integrating music technology into instruction is almost always a teacher-initiated process, as it should be. The process of a professional educator's examining and implementing technology tools in a manner best suited to his or her students can and should be an empowering experience for the teacher. The information in this book provides a starting point for this process, but the central ingredient will always be you.

Feeling stuck or overwhelmed? Start with this needs-assessment checklist.

Music Technology Integration Needs Assessment		Details Known	More Information Needed
Who?	Who are your students? What is their age and technology experience level?		
	Do any students need assistive or adaptive technologies?		
	Who are the stakeholders?		
	What are the expectations of the school and community?		
	Is there an instructional technology plan in place, or do you need to gain buy-in from school officials and parents?		
	What is your comfort level with technology? How about your colleagues?		
What?	What are you trying to teach? Music performance? Music theory? Composition? Music listening and critique? Technology skills?		
	What resources do you already have? Are computers, tablets, Chromebooks, microphones, recording devices, document cameras, and other items already available? Check with your school IT staff, instructional coaches, and media specialists. Check through all of your "old" gear, too. If it has a MIDI, USB, or XLR connection, it may be usable.		
	What devices can your students use? Does every student have device like an iPad tablet or Chromebook? Can you borrow a cart with devices or use a technology lab?		
	Does your school have a BYOD (Bring Your Own Device) policy allowing students to use their own smartphones and other devices?		
	What software, LMSs, or subscriptions do you already have?		
	What's the budget now, and what is the planned spending for the next 5–8 years?		
Where?	Will students be able to use technology in your regular classroom, or is another space like a lab needed?		
	Do you have space and electrical outlets to install computer workstations?		
	Where will you store gear like microphones, stands, and interface boxes?		
	How robust and reliable is the WiFi in your classroom?		
	Do you expect students to use technology for music class at home? Do they have access to devices and Internet/WiFi connection outside of school? If not, find out whether your school can loan devices to students overnight, or if students can get free access at a public library or community center. The "digital divide" between the "haves" and "have-nots" is a legitimate concern, and we need to ensure that no student is put at an educational disadvantage for economic reasons.		

Music Technology Integration Needs Assessment	Details Known	More Information Needed
When? How often do you hope to use technology yourself as part of instruction or assessment? Every teacher does a balancing act between music making and other instructional and assessment activities.		
How often do you expect students to be hands-on with technology? Maximizing rehearsal time is important, and your choices of technology can help make rehearsal time more efficient.		
How much time (in minutes) do you anticipate students will need technology for each type of activity? Will they use tech frequently in short spurts, or for the bulk of a class period from time to time? Be sure to plan for some extra time when you first introduce a technology-based music activity. There are always a few glitches to resolve, and students will need time to walk through initial access or login steps.		
Is there a longer-term plan? What growth in class size and offerings can you foresee over the next 5 or 10 years?		
Why? Are you trying to meet some state mandate or local technology plan?		
Are you attempting to stay current and relevant?		
Are you looking for a way to connect with kids whose brains are wired differently?		
Do you seek to meet the needs of ever-more-diverse student populations?		

Glossary

This glossary is provided as a resource for readers who may be new to music education technology. Most of these terms are discussed in the main text. This section is intended as a general reference only, and should not be regarded as legal, policy, or purchasing advice.

Educational Technology Acronyms

BYOD.
: Bring Your Own Device. Many schools have specific policies and procedures outlining permissible use of personal devices including smartphones, laptops, Chromebooks, and tablets during the school day. These policies also govern student access to school WiFi networks.

COPPA.
: Children's Online Privacy and Protection Act. US legislation passed in 1998 that requires parental consent for collection of any information about Internet users under age thirteen and precludes the collection of user data without consent.

CIPA.
: Children's Internet Protection Act. US legislation enacted in 2000 that requires educational institutions receiving E- rate funding to utilize filters and firewalls to protect students from inappropriate material.

FERPA.
: Family Educational Rights and Privacy Act. US legislation in effect since 1974 that requires all educational institutions to safeguard the identities of students, including college and university students.

FOIA.
: Freedom of Information Act. US federal legislation allowing members of the public to request documents and records of communications. Several US states have enacted similar legislation with the same name, or as Open Public Records Acts (OPRA). At the state level, such legislation requires that public schools have the ability to access written and electronic communications between staff members and students.

GDPR.
: General Data Protection Regulation. Passed by the EU in 2016, GDPR compliance requires provide safeguards to protect user data, and that users of websites and apps must explicitly agree to the collection of data as set forth

in the electronic platform's privacy policy (informed consent). Nearly all web platforms comply with this standard.

LMS. Learning Management Systems are online platforms that include virtual classrooms, instructional materials, discussion forums, assessment tools, gradebooks, and messaging systems.

LTI. Learning Tool Interoperability is an educational technology standard used by application developers to ensure that their products communicate and share data properly within Learning Management Systems (LMSs).

OPRA. Open Public Records Act. Several US states provide mechanisms for public records requests in line with the federal Freedom of Information Act (FOIA). Communications within publicly funded institutions such as schools may be subject to an OPRA request, therefore schools are required to be able to access all written and electronic communications between staff members and students.

SAMR. Substitution, Augmentation, Modification, and Redefinition. Developed by Ruben Puentedura, SAMR examines technology use in the context of past teaching practice.

STEAM. Science, Technology Engineering, Arts, Mathematics. The STEAM approach to education uses the integration of these five disciplines in an integrated manner to foster student inquiry and critical thinking, and to engage in project-based learning.

SSO. Single Sign On. Password management systems used in schools and corporations to unify and manage user access to multiple applications.

TPACK. Technology, Pedagogy and Content Knowledge. Developed by Matthew Koehler and Punya Mishra, TPACK explores the interaction between technological practice, pedagogical practice, and content knowledge.

Music Technology Terms and Acronyms

Channel. Input or output pathway. Most recording programs allow multiple input channels, but limit output to two channels, left and right for *stereo* sound.

DAW. Digital Audio Workstation. These multi-track recording programs accommodate audio recordings and MIDI tracks. Some advanced DAWs include music notation display and editing.

Drum Machine. Automated percussion device or application. Commonly, drum machines employ a 16-column grid for sequencing 1 measure of common time with sixteenth note subdivisions. Each row of the grid represents one percussion sound, such as kick drum, snare, or closed high hat. Hardware-based drum machines emerged in the 1980's. Software-based drum machines are common today.

Effects. Audio elements such as reverb, chorus, EQ and filtering that are often added after recording in a DAW or other recording program.

Fades. Changes in volume level as the music progresses. In DAWs, fades often are displayed as line graphs associated with individual tracks.

Levels. Volume. In audio recording, level checks ensure that the input volume is appropriate to the overall recording environment. When input levels are too high, *clipping* may result, as the ends of the audio waveform exceed capacity and are "clipped off."

MIDI. Musical Instrument Digital Interface. Developed in the 1980's, the MIDI standard allows communication of musical information as a type of computer code. MIDI is the protocol used in much music software, applications, and for hardware, such as digital instruments and sound cards. Use of this standard creates compatibility across software applications and hardware devices.

Pan. Short for *panorama*, pan is volume adjustment more to the left, right or evenly "up the middle" to both left and right when using standard stereo output. In DAWs, pan adjustment is often displayed with line graphs associated with individual tracks, as well as with a knob or slider governing the entire track.

Region. Block of musical content, either audio or midi data. Regions are stored in *tracks*.

Track. Where music is stored in a DAW or recording program. Typically, tracks are represented horizontally, with music progressing left to right, as in a musical score. Items which align vertically occur at the same time. Finished musical recordings are also referred to as tracks.

Index

Tables and figures are indicated by *t* and *f* following the page number

For the benefit of digital users, indexed terms that span two pages (e.g., 52–53) may, on occasion, appear on only one of those pages.